Images of America
La Crescenta

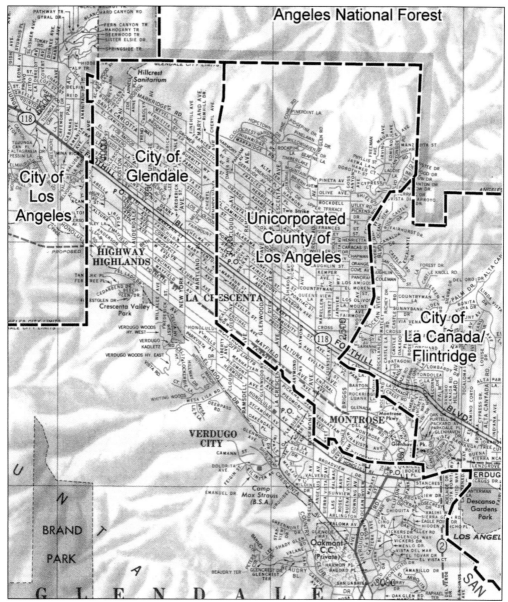

This map from the late 1960s (before the freeways cut across the landscape) is overlaid with the current civic boundaries, illustrating the complexities of the political divisions of the area that was once known simply as La Crescenta. Although the valley is clearly geographically defined, annexations and incorporations have divided it among four governments. This book focuses on what today is unincorporated La Crescenta, but the area's story transcends political boundaries.

ON THE COVER: This 1913 photograph of Crescenta Valley was taken by B. D. Jackson, a La Cañada resident who shot many of the early panoramas in this book. At the time, Jackson was known more for his illegal "jitney" taxi service than for his photographs. The orchard in the foreground is the current site of Glendale College. The unfinished Cañada Boulevard run through the center, next to the tracks of the Glendale and Montrose Railway just before they were extended to Montrose.

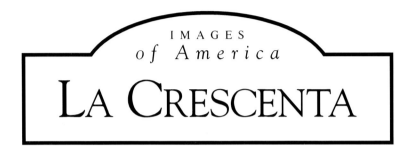

IMAGES of America
LA CRESCENTA

Mike Lawler and Robert Newcombe

Copyright © 2005 by Mike Lawler and Robert Newcombe
ISBN 978-0-7385-3074-1

Published by Arcadia Publishing
Charleston, South Carolina

Printed in the United States of America

Library of Congress Catalog Card Number: 2005932379

For all general information contact Arcadia Publishing at:
Telephone 843-853-2070
Fax 843-853-0044
E-mail sales@arcadiapublishing.com
For customer service and orders:
Toll-Free 1-888-313-2665

Visit us on the Internet at www.arcadiapublishing.com

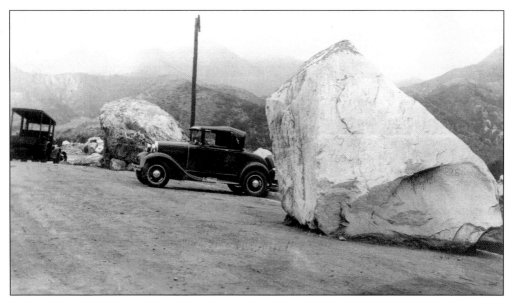

In La Crescenta, the spreading suburbs of Los Angeles have run up hard against one of the most geologically dynamic mountain ranges in the world. The San Gabriel Mountains, known as the Sierra Madres until the 1920s, have regularly rained down mud and rocks, hurricane-force winds, and unstoppable firestorms on the peaceful Crescenta Valley. In just a few minutes on New Year's Day 1934, a flash flood roared out of the mountains and decimated the community below. The flow of water and debris was so strong, these immense boulders were picked up and deposited on the street near the top of New York Avenue.

Contents

Acknowledgments		6
Introduction		7
1.	Before It Was La Crescenta	11
2.	Early La Crescenta	17
3.	Tourism and Health Seekers	31
4.	Shacks and Castles	41
5.	Daily Life	53
6.	The Wonder and Fury of Nature	75
7.	The Good, the Sad, and the Seedy	95
8.	The Shift from Rural to Suburban	117

ACKNOWLEDGMENTS

This book is only meant to be a taste of the dynamic history of the Crescenta Valley and not a comprehensive narrative. We have had to omit, because of space limitations or bad timing, many critical portions of the past, most regrettably some record of the thousand years of human presence of the Tongva people. Their stories are nearly lost now and to have missed this chance to record them is sad indeed. The most painful part of writing this book was cutting out hundreds of photographs and editing out all the stories that space would not allow. And since this is a photographic history, we had to leave out some events for which we didn't have related photographs. (When you read it, you'll see we had to stretch a few times to tie the photograph with the caption.)

We are especially indebted to the people who have preserved the history of La Crescenta. A few years ago, author June Dougherty compiled a book of La Crescenta history that, unlike our book, is comprehensive and indexed, so that looking up facts and dates was relatively easy. Under the guidance of the Carpenter family, *The Ledger*, the local newspaper from the 1920s to the 1980s, had a soft spot for local history and recorded much of the past in their pages. Art Cobery, a local historian, has done a great service to the community by single-handedly getting all issues of *The Ledger* recorded on microfilm for viewing at our neighborhood libraries, as well as recording his own investigations into events of the past. The members of the Historical Society of the Crescenta Valley have contributed much to the preservation of our historical heritage by their enthusiasm and contributions of artifacts, memories, time, and money.

Huge thanks to the three librarians who have assisted us and loaned us materials: George Ellison of the Special Collections Room at the Glendale Central Library, Vicki Guagliardo of the La Crescenta Library, and Judy Hoeptner of the Montrose Library.

And thanks to Maureen Pallaccio, owner of Once Upon A Time Bookstore in Montrose, for kick-starting this whole project.

Special thanks to our families for putting up with us during this project, especially to Deborah Newcombe for (involuntarily) giving up a corner of her kitchen for months to store photographs, papers, and equipment.

We appreciate the many photographs and stories that members of the community have allowed us to use. As they have given us that gift, we will give back to the community, and all royalties from this book will be donated to the Historical Society of the Crescenta Valley.

Unless otherwise noted, photographs in this book are from the archives of the Historical Society of the Crescenta Valley. No photographs in this book may be reproduced without permission of the owner.

INTRODUCTION

The Crescenta Valley descends from the San Gabriel Mountains on the north, the Los Angeles city communities of Sunland and Tujunga on the west, Glendale on the south, and La Cañada on the east.

For thousands of years, the Tongva (also known as the Gabrieleno) Indians inhabited the valley. Evidence has been found to indicate that permanent villages existed in La Tuna Canyon, Big Tujunga Cayon, and the Devil's Gate Dam area. It's likely that villages also existed in Las Barras Canyon, Pickens Canyon, and the Indian Springs area east of Montrose. The American Indians lived prosperously and peacefully in the valley until the arrival of the Spanish in the late 1700s. Cattle grazing, the establishment of the San Fernando Mission to the west, the San Gabriel Mission to the east, and the trail connecting them spelled doom for the Tongva people, who virtually disappeared from the area by the early 1800s.

In 1784, King Charles III of Spain granted 36,000 acres that included the Crescenta Valley to one of his corporals, Don Jose Maria Verdugo (for whom the mountains on the west end of the valley are named). Verdugo used the land for cattle and sheep grazing while he continued to fight for Spain, stationed at the San Gabriel Mission. After he was honorably discharged, he moved to the rancho, which he called La Zanja (but was officially known as Rancho San Rafael). Verdugo died in 1831, and his children continued to live and raise livestock in the valley.

After America took over California in 1848, the Verdugos' claim to the property was disputed by the new government. The first "American" to settle in the valley was Col. Theodore Pickens, a Civil War veteran, who established a homestead in 1871, claiming ownership of what is now called Pickens Canyon and Briggs Terrace. To make a living, he sold water rights and logging rights to the tall trees at the top of the lush canyon.

In 1875, Dr. Jacob Lanterman and a partner purchased 5,830 acres of Rancho La Cañada, which they divided into 46 large lots. In 1881, Dr. Benjamin Briggs conducted a worldwide search for the ideal healthful climate and settled on the Crescenta Valley for his new family. (Briggs' first wife had died of tuberculosis; he married her sister.) Briggs bought Colonel Pickens' homestead and then the entire valley, from Pickens Canyon west to Tujunga.

Dr. Briggs named the area Crescenta, but there is some dispute on what inspired the name. Some claim that he looked out the window of his house and could see three crescents in the landscape; others claim that the crescent is formed by the way the points of the valley stretch around the hills into the mountains. And since "Crescenta" is not a Spanish word, no one is sure if he made it up or perhaps borrowed it from another language (such as Italian). The U.S. Post Office supposedly added the "La" to distinguish it from Crescent City up north.

What is not disputed is that Briggs created a master plan for the Crescenta Valley, laying out streets and designating the intersection of (what are now) Foothill Boulevard and La Crescenta Avenue as the town center. He split his subdivision into parallelogram-shaped, 10-acre lots.

During this time, Briggs opened a sanitarium for people with respiratory ailments (asthma especially) and soon health seekers flocked to the area in search of that same ideal climate—both the clean air and clear drinking water. Success bred imitation, and other sanitariums followed, such as the Kimball and Rockhaven Sanitariums.

Wealthy health seekers built mansions (and even two castles) in the area, while average wage earners lived in shacks and small bungalows. Many of the new arrivals were immigrants. They planted olive and fruit trees and grape vines. The Crescenta Valley shifted from livestock grazing to farming, but its main industry was tourism. Tourists were attracted by the mountains, clean air, and the Gould Castle. There were two hotels, and people made the stagecoach trip from Pasadena, which was a tourism capital at the time with its orange groves, the Rose Parade, and entrance to the Mount Lowe railroad that took visitors up the mountainside.

Helen Haskell Thomas, Briggs' niece, helped found the first school in La Crescenta, which opened in 1886, with Mrs. Thomas the first teacher. The population expanded rapidly and a new school had to be built within a few years. Helen's husband, Seymour Thomas, was a world-famous portrait artist. After the two of them tired of globe-trotting, they settled down in the Crescenta Valley. They had weekly Sunday teas at their home which attracted the rich and famous of the Los Angeles area. Thomas painted what he imagined a stone church should look like and a local parish built it based on that painting. The church was St. Luke's and soon became the landmark of the valley.

In 1912, electricity came to the neighborhood. Developers laid out the area south of Foothill Boulevard in the shape of a rose and called the new subdivision Montrose (as in Mountain Rose). The business district was supposed to cut through the middle of the rose along Montrose Avenue, but instead formed along Honolulu Avenue, at the bottom (and less hilly) end of the rose. While the lots sold spectacularly on the opening day, the area floundered until the economic boom of the 1920s, which brought increased building in the valley. As was the practice in many parts of California at the time, racial covenants were included in property deeds that kept non-whites from owning land in the area.

By then, the two hotels had closed, the Gould castle was no longer a big attraction, the air had lost some of its cleanliness, and tourists no longer flocked to the area. But with electric trolleys and good roads extending to downtown Los Angeles, the area started the shift from a farming community to being a suburb.

The one-room schoolhouse had to be expanded, but La Crescenta, being unincorporated, did not have the resources to build and run both an elementary school and a high school so they made a deal with the City of Glendale, which took responsibility for the schools in 1931.

In 1932, the City of Los Angeles claimed a piece of the Crescenta Valley when it annexed Tujunga (as a continuation of its annexation of almost the entire San Fernando Valley).

Like everywhere during the Great Depression, the Crescenta Valley stagnated in the early 1930s. Businesses went under. A horrendous flash flood carrying mud, boulders, and other debris rolled down from the mountains on New Year's Day 1934, killing dozens, destroying many homes, and leaving the area reeling. In response, the Army Corps of Engineers devised a series of concrete channels and "debris basins" in the hopes of preventing further such incidents. Some local residents argued against the ugly and unproven basins, but they were built over the objections.

In the late 1930s, Americans styling themselves after German Nazis held several rallies at Hindenburg Park (now Crescenta Valley Park). After the United States entered the war, many of these Nazi sympathizers were imprisoned at a detention camp in the western end of the valley.

During World War II, many servicemen discovered the wonders of California and, after the war, moved there. Many fell in love with the quiet of the Crescenta Valley and its close proximity to Los Angeles, finding it an ideal place to raise a family. Orchards, vineyards, and open land disappeared as houses were built on all the lots that had been laid out by Briggs and Montrose developers years before. The City of Glendale kept pace by building or expanding schools to keep up with the ever increasing number of children living in the valley.

As a result of the increased population, though, the area was running out of the clean drinking water that came from the mountains above the valley. Sewage was becoming a problem as septic tanks reached the ends of their life cycles and there was not enough percolatable land to build new ones. In 1948, concerned residents of the area broached the subject of annexation with the City of Glendale. The matter was voted on near the end of 1949 and soundly lost. Supporters of the plan did not give up and citizen groups in different pockets of the valley managed to get annexation on the ballot once again. On December 11, 1951, voters in the areas of Montrose, Verdugo City, Whiting Woods, Highway Highlands, and other sections approved the annexation.

(It was these different petitioning groups that caused La Crescenta to become politically split with the confusing boundaries between what is now Glendale and unincorporated La Crescenta today.) In 1964, a vote was taken to incorporate what's left of La Crescenta, but the measure was soundly defeated—4,149 to 813. In 1976, the area to the east was incorporated as La Cañada–Flintridge, leaving only a portion of what used to be La Crescenta as "unincorporated La Crescenta." Every few years, someone tries to make what's left of La Crescenta incorporated, but so far, residents do not seem interested.

Enforcement of racial covenants was outlawed by the Supreme Court in 1953, and non-whites started buying property in the valley. However, a few white supremacists who remained in the area tried to bring the Ku Klux Klan to the valley. While no one stopped them, few joined.

As the number of cars increased in the area, the once spectacularly clean air was replaced by smog. Ironically the sons and daughters of those health seekers who had moved to the Crescenta Valley to cure their lung ailments now suffered through summers of aching lungs, stinging eyes, and a brown haze that often obscured the San Gabriel mountains. Automobile emission rules imposed by the state and county in the last 40 years have significantly reduced smog in the valley.

In the 1960s, against intense opposition from citizens, businesses, and local civic leaders, the state of California planned to crisscross the valley with two freeways—the 210 running east and west, and the 2 running north and south. Whenever anyone who lived in the planned path put their home on the market, the state bought it, leaving the houses empty rather than renting them out. Eventually the state had to use eminent domain to buy the rest of the houses. Construction was started in 1969, and the first leg of the Foothill Freeway (210) opened in July 1972. The extension connecting it to the I-5 in the west was opened in 1981, and the Glendale Freeway (2) was completed in 1978.

As the Crescenta Valley became more crowded and built-up in the 1960s, local officials realized that careful planning would be necessary in the future, especially with the Foothill Freeway tearing through the heart of the area. Since much of the valley was still unincorporated, responsibility for the planning lay with the Los Angeles County Regional Planners Commission and the Board of Supervisors. Noting the earlier votes and residents' outspoken feelings about preserving the rural qualities, the planning commission and citizens committee decided on a plan with these words setting the tone: "The Crescenta Valley is not destined to become a center of employment or commerce . . . La Crescenta will continue to fill the vital role of a predominately residential community." Forty years later, those words still ring true.

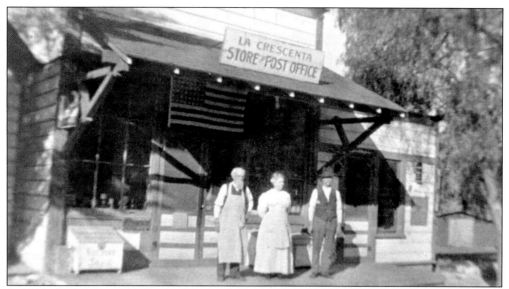

In 1895, the La Crescenta General Store and Post Office was the "downtown" of La Crescenta. The intersection of Los Angeles and Michigan (today La Crescenta and Foothill) had been chosen by founder Dr. Benjamin Briggs as the "city center," boasting a stage-stop, school, church, and city park. But La Crescenta never quite became a "city," and the city center lost its focus. (Courtesy Glendale Library.)

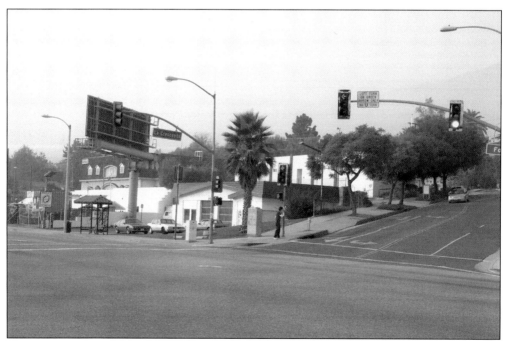

That intersection today shows nothing of its former promise, looking as bland as almost every other block of Foothill. (This is where the Holly House stood for many years; see page 22.) However, there is hope for a rebirth of the city center. Years of lobbying by civic groups and the Crescenta Valley Town Council have paid off, as this neglected corner will soon become the site of a new large library and community center.

One
BEFORE IT WAS LA CRESCENTA

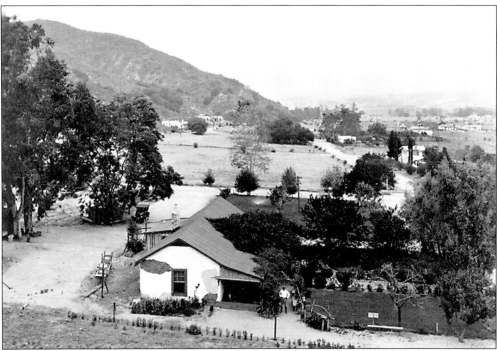

The Tongva (or Gabrielino) Indians inhabited the Crescenta Valley peacefully for thousands of years, but were forced out of the area in 1784 when the Spanish government granted Cpl. Don Jose Maria Verdugo 36,000 acres that included all of the valley. Verdugo didn't live there (the valley was considered almost uninhabitable), but his family raised and grazed cattle, sheep, and horses. When he died in 1831, his children inherited the land, building homes in different areas of the rancho. In 1860, Verdugo's grandson Teodoro built this adobe, shown here in 1911, looking north up Verdugo Canyon toward the Crescenta Valley. His daughter Dora Verdugo was born in this adobe in 1882 and attended the little one-room La Crescenta schoolhouse. The adobe passed out of the hands of the Verdugo family in the early 1900s but is still in existence, serving as a museum operated by the City of Glendale. (Courtesy Glendale Library.)

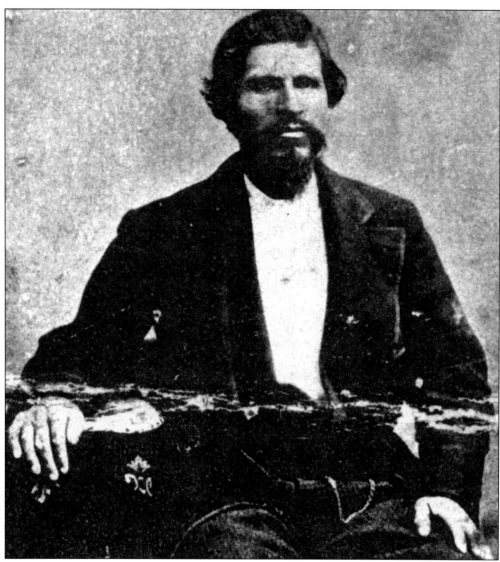

Tiburcio Vasquez was a bandit who plied his "trade" throughout California from 1852 to 1874. In 1873, Vasquez moved to Southern California and hid out in the San Gabriel Mountains and an area of Soledad Canyon now known as Vasquez Rocks. In 1874, Vasquez and his men camped at the base of the Arroyo Seco then overtook a wealthy man named Repetto on his ranch in what is now Monterey Park. Sheriff Billy Rowland quickly organized a posse and chased Vasquez and his men up the Arroyo Seco wash into the mountains. Nightfall stopped them, but the chase continued in the morning with the bandits racing to the end of the crest trail above Crescenta Valley. They headed almost straight down into the chaparral toward what is now Tujunga. Vasquez's horse stumbled into a deep gully and broke its leg, but the outlaw managed to leap off. Vasquez continued on foot, carrying his saddle and two guns. At some point, he left the saddle and one gun behind. He managed to escape, but was caught in what is now Hollywood on May 13, 1874. On March 19, 1875, he was hung for his crimes.

In 1972, Star Barnum stood on the Old Soledad Road, the valley's first road, just before freeway construction covered it. In 1871, Mormon engineers, needing a wagon route to transport silver from the Mojave Desert, carved out the road through the Verdugo Canyon into Montrose and then diagonally across La Cañada to the Angeles Crest. They stopped work when a railroad was built, but pieces of the old road can still be found in the San Gabriels.

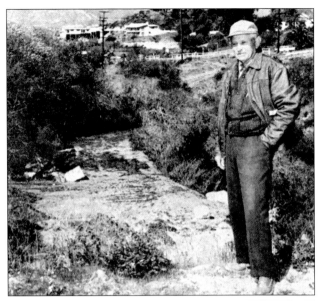

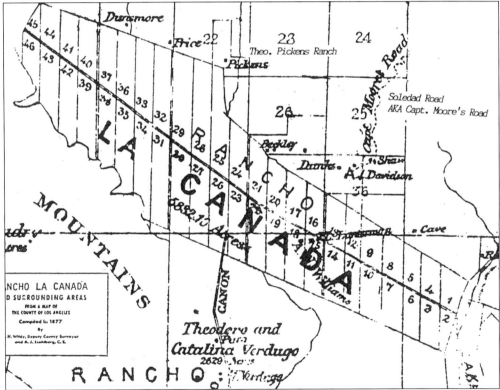

Soon after the United States acquired California, many of the ranchos owned by Californios were taken by American lawyers in exchange for legal fees. In 1852, attorney Benjamin Hayes took ownership of the Crescenta-Cañada Valley. It passed through various hands and was sold in 1876 to Jacob Lanterman and Colonel Williams, who divided the property into the 100-acre lots shown above. In 1881, Benjamin Briggs purchased the western half of the land. (Courtesy June Dougherty.)

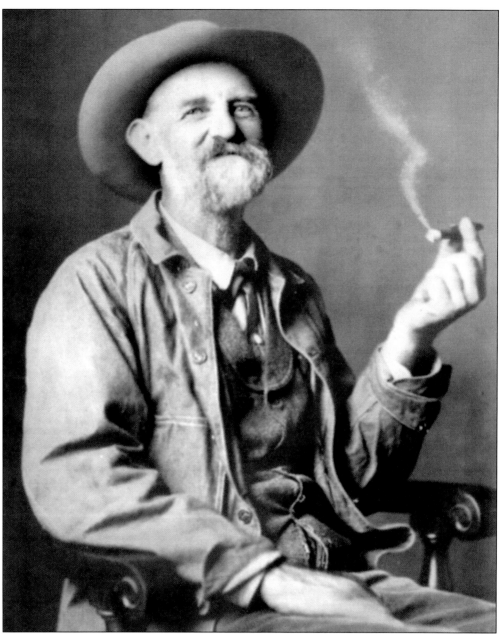

In 1871, Theodore Pickens filed for the first homestead in the Crescenta Valley, claiming the land on (what is now) Briggs Terrace, above the Rancho La Cañada boundary and water and timber rights to the canyon that now bears his name. The home that allowed him to claim all this was a simple, one-room shack. Pickens claimed that he was a Kentuckian who fought in the Civil War for the Union side and that he earned the title of colonel. However, a modern-day check of Civil War enlistment records shows only a Theodore Pickens in an Illinois regiment, who was dismissed with a disability in training camp. When the Williams and Lantermans bought the rancho land below Pickens, they were without a steady water source. Although they openly called Pickens a "squatter," they were forced to buy water rights from him in 1878 for $1,250. Pickens sold timber rights to woodcutters from Los Angeles. In 1881, he sold his homestead to Dr. Briggs.

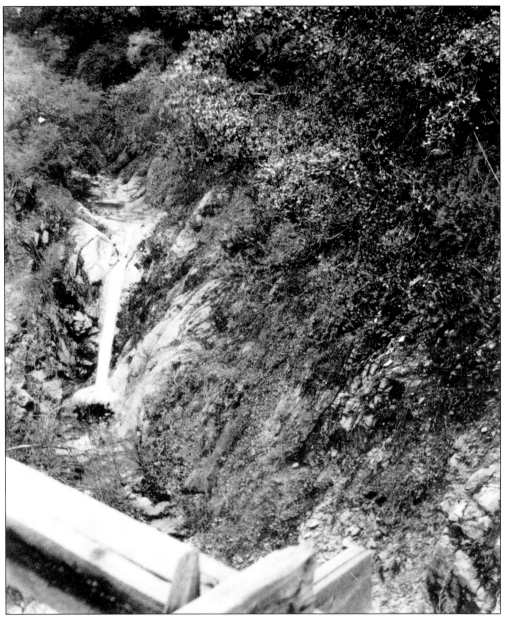

This photograph of a waterfall in Pickens Canyon was taken over 100 years ago from the train trestle that crossed Mullally Canyon. In the early 1880s, the growing city of Los Angeles needed fuel for its burgeoning industries. Mr. Mullally of the Mullally Brick Company and his foremen, the Blaine Brothers, filed timber claims to the east of Pickens Canyon. At that time, the canyons were heavily forested with Big Cone Douglas Fir trees, many four to five feet in diameter. A rail tramway was installed, and each summer a crew of Chinese felled the trees, cutting them into four-foot lengths, which they stacked on a small railcar. With one man on the brakes, the car rolled down the rails to Briggs' barn, where the wood was loaded on wagons for the trip to the downtown brick kilns. It wasn't long before the timber supplies were exhausted. The rail line was abandoned, but later used by the Bathey children as a thrill ride with their own homemade railcar. (Courtesy Glendale Library.)

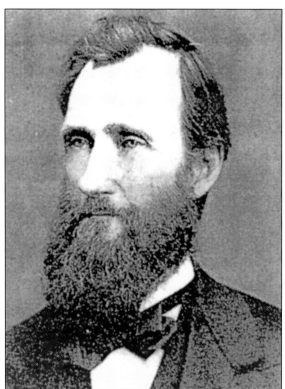

Shortly after the subdivision of Rancho La Cañada, Dr. Benjamin Briggs bought most of the rancho west of Pickens Canyon, covering most of the Crescenta Valley (including Montrose) except for a small strip in Tujunga. Because of the shape of the area with its "points" into the mountain, he called it Crescenta, a word he made up. The post office supposedly added the "La" to distinguish it from Crescent City (in northern California). Briggs made innumerable contributions to the valley and died here on February 15, 1893.

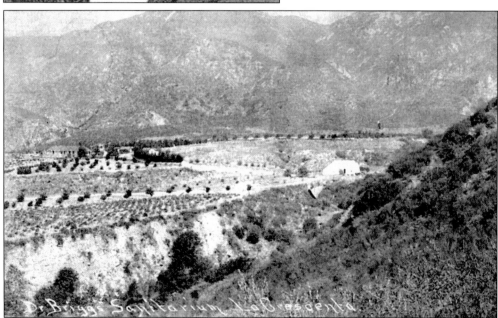

In 1881, Dr. Benjamin Briggs established his sanitarium. Looking northwest from what is now the top of Ocean View after the turn of the 20th century, Briggs house is the wide building on the left, the sanitarium is the structure surrounded by trees, and his whitewashed barn is on the right. Briggs loved trees and planted the many orchards and vineyards on his land. Legend has it that Briggs could see the crescent of the valley from this terrace. (Courtesy Bill Swisher.)

Two

EARLY LA CRESCENTA

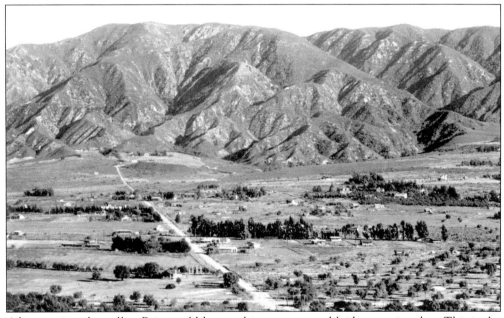

After naming the valley, Briggs sold lots on his property and laid out a city plan. This is the Crescenta Valley as seen from the Verdugo Mountains almost 30 years later. Prominent are the lines of eucalyptus trees planted along the east-west roadways as windbreaks to the fierce winds that were more common in the early years of La Crescenta. A few homes and ranches have been carved out of the sagebrush, but the majority of the valley remains untamed. The boom years would come later. The main north-south street in the valley was Los Angeles Street (now La Crescenta Avenue) running up the valley to a cleared area at the base of the San Gabriels, which was by this period owned by the Bissell family, of the Bissell Carpet Sweeper Company. (Courtesy Glendale Library.)

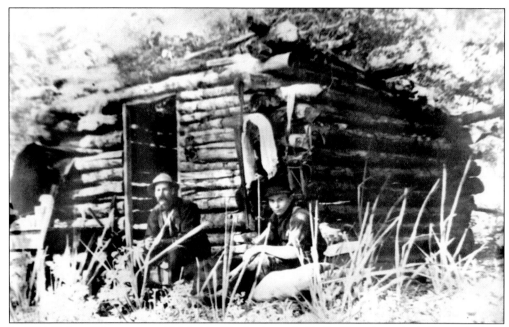

In 1884, Robert Waterman and his bride, Elizabeth, settled in La Cañada in the hills overlooking Montrose. His health failed, so they packed their belongings on a mule and headed into the mountains. In 1897, Rob Waterman and his brother-in-law relax at their cabin near Switzers Camp. The Watermans returned to the Crescenta Valley in 1900, but not before having Mount Waterman, Waterman Canyon, and Waterman Ranger Station named for them. (Courtesy Glendale Library.)

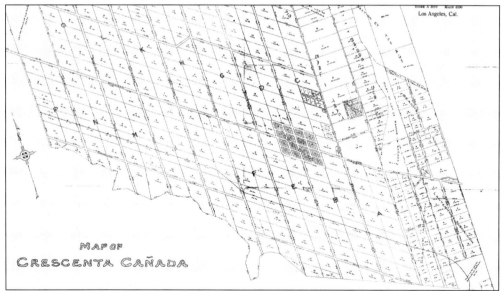

In 1884, Briggs mapped out parallelogram-shaped, 14-acre lots for La Crescenta. The top and bottom boundaries of the lots ran parallel to Michigan Avenue (Foothill Boulevard), with the side boundaries parallel to Los Angeles Street (La Crescenta Avenue). The dark area at the intersection of Michigan Avenue and Los Angeles Street was the planned city center. This map from 1910 predates the rose-patterned street layout of Montrose.

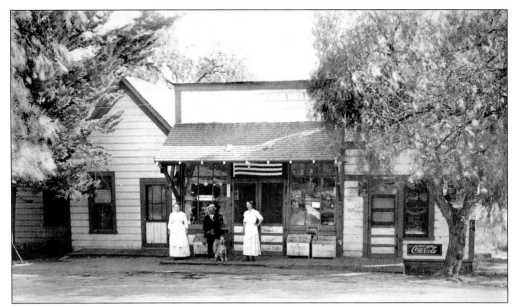

At the southeast corner of Michigan Avenue (Foothill Boulevard) and Los Angeles Street (La Crescenta Avenue), in the central business district of La Crescenta, Mr. Weatherbee poses with two female companions and his dog on the front porch of his grocery store and post office about 1912. Electricity has just been installed, the first in the valley, as evidenced by the light bulb just above the door. (Courtesy Glendale Library.)

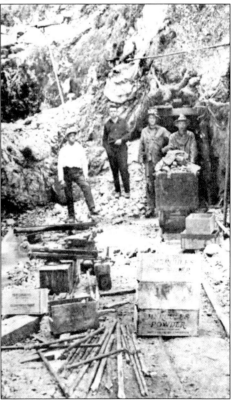

With the population growing, runoff water from Pickens Canyon was no longer enough. Miners, using mostly hand tools and some dynamite, tunneled horizontally hundreds of feet to water-bearing fissures in the San Gabriels, dumping the rubble into ore carts that they had to push out. This 1917 photograph shows miners working at the mouth of the Pickens well, which still produces tens of thousands of gallons a day for the residents of Crescenta Valley.

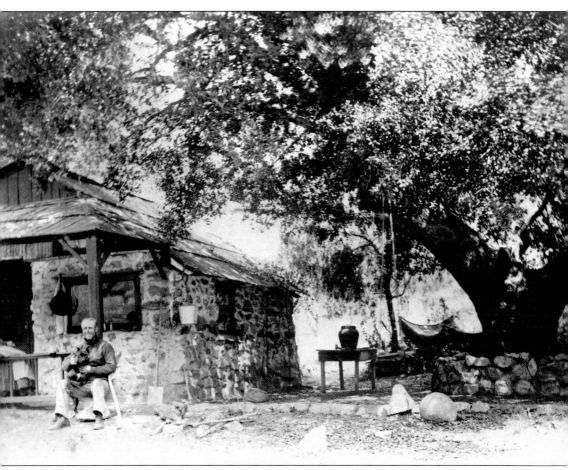

Las Barras Canyon used to contain a flowing spring, which undoubtedly made it the site of a seasonal Tongva village. In the 1700s, when the route between the San Gabriel and San Fernando Missions lay through the Crescenta Valley, the spring at Las Barras Canyon was a halfway stopping point for travelers. This route was later known as Horse-Thief Pass because it was used by so many banditos driving their stolen horses from Los Angeles to their corrals in the canyons of the San Gabriels. When the Begue family moved to Las Barras Canyon in the early 1880s, they reported that a stone-lined well existed in the canyon with the remains of a decayed adobe wall next to it. The Begues built a stone house on the property, shown here, one of the first in the valley. In the 1930s, the government bought the land and set up a Civilian Conservation Corps (CCC) camp there. It is now the site of the Verdugo Hills Golf Course.

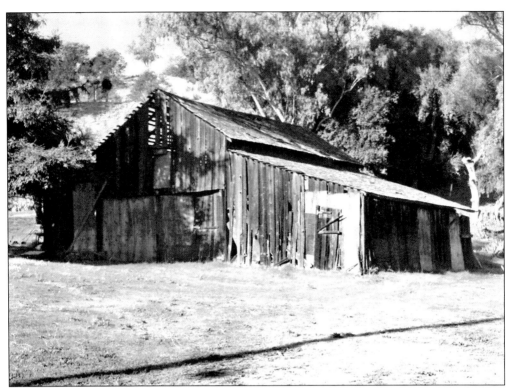

The Begue family built this barn on their land at the extreme west end of the valley. The family grew grapes and fruit trees, kept bees, and even ran a little barbecue restaurant on Foothill Boulevard. The barn stood just south of Tujunga Canyon Road for over 100 years, a link to the Crescenta Valley's past. In 2004, the property owners demolished it.

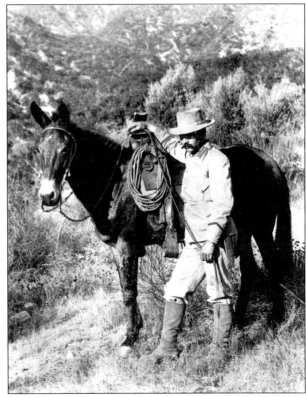

La Crescenta pioneer Phil Begue was a San Gabriel Timberland Reserve Ranger, the first National Forest Rangers. When he was 16, Phil Begue found the pistol and saddle (now at the L.A. County Museum) that had been discarded by bandit Vasquez in the mountains above La Crescenta during his last escape attempt in 1874. (Courtesy John Robinson.)

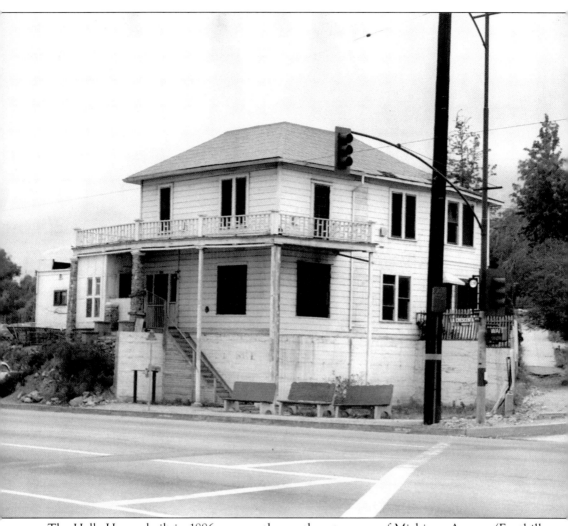

The Holly House, built in 1886, was on the northwest corner of Michigan Avenue (Foothill Boulevard) and Los Angeles Street (La Crescenta Avenue). The Holly family of Elgin, Illinois, after the death of one child and the poor health of Mrs. Holly, joined the throng of health seekers coming to the area for the restorative climate. Mr. Holly was an engineer and inventor and the beautiful eight-room home he built featured indoor plumbing and a hot water system. In a terrible windstorm one night in 1890, the La Crescenta Hotel blew down, and Mr. Holly was the first on the scene to help pull the dead and injured from the wreckage. The last remaining piece of Crescenta Valley's town center, the Holly House was many things in the remainder of its life, including being the location of the Crescenta-Cañada YMCA. In 1962, it was torn down to make way for a gas station. There are plans to build a new library and community center on the site. (Courtesy Glendale Library.)

In 1888, Helen Haskell was visiting her uncle Benjamin Briggs when he asked her to teach the first class of their community's proposed school for a couple of weeks until they could hire a teacher. She became the first teacher of La Crescenta Elementary School. (She did the same thing for La Cañada Elementary School.) She later married artist Seymour Thomas and became a major socialite in the valley. (Courtesy Witte Museum.)

In 1886, "Villa Esperanza" was built on the southeast corner of Foothill Boulevard and Rosemont for Professor White, retiring president of Wabash College in Indiana. Professor White had edited the novel *Ben Hur* for author Lew Wallace, who was his first guest, followed by other rich and famous people of that era. Villa Esperanza became the center of culture for the valley. Later it was the rectory of St. Luke's Church across the street. (Courtesy Frank Boyer.)

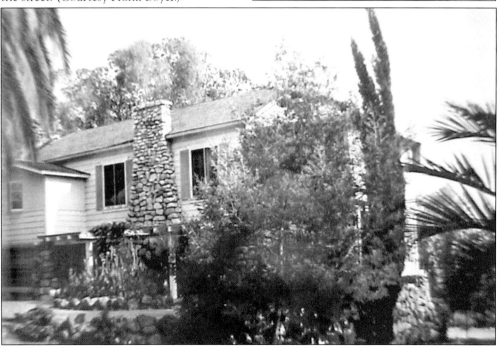

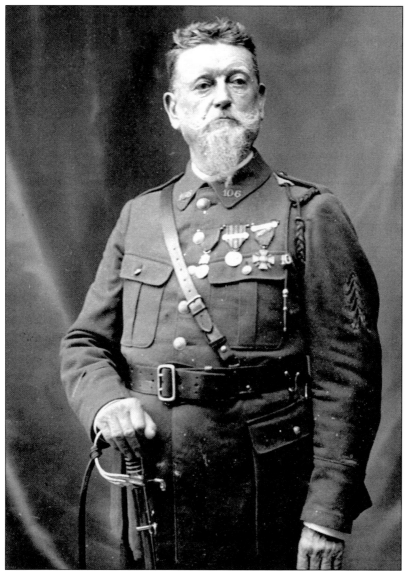

The colorful Frenchman George Le Mesnager moved to California from New York, but promptly returned to France in 1870 to fight in the Franco-Prussian War. After his beloved homeland lost the war, Le Mesnager came back to Southern California and tried a little of everything. He grazed sheep, opened a French market in downtown Los Angeles, planted grapevines in Glendale and other locations, worked as a county court translator, edited a French newspaper, and finally started a winery using grapes that he grew. His winery, located in downtown Los Angeles at Main and Mesnager Street (named after George), produced well-regarded wines. As his business grew, Le Mesnager bought more land, including a large section in La Crescenta. During World War I at the age of 64, Le Mesnager returned once again to fight for France, enlisting as a private since he was too old to be an officer. He was wounded five times, returned to Los Angeles to recuperate, and then went back to France to fight again. He won three medals, including the Legion of Honor and the Croix de Guerre. After the war, he came back to La Crescenta, only to have his wine business put under by Prohibition. After suffering a stroke, Le Mesnager and his wife returned to France in 1921, where he died two years later at the age of 72. (Courtesy Denice Spanwick.)

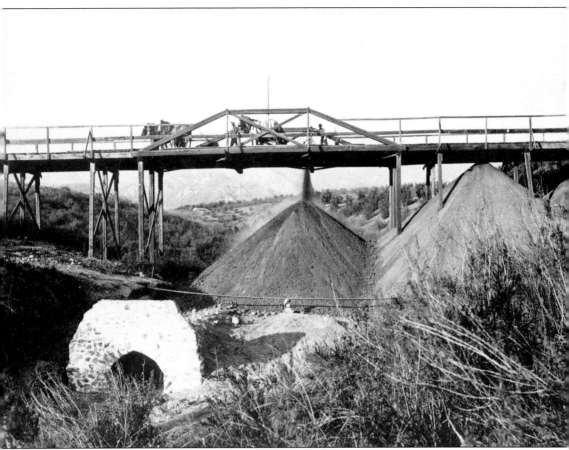

When Foothill Boulevard (then Michigan Avenue) was first laid out as a straight road by Edward Haskell in the late 1800s, it had to traverse many canyons and gullies that interrupted the valley floor. To make a manageable road, wooden trestles were built across some of the ravines, the largest being at Hilliard Avenue in La Cañada. But the trestles were hard to maintain so in 1901, the ravines were filled by dumping dirt off the bridge from wagons until the fill reached the level of the bridge roadway. Foothill Boulevard was finally paved in the late 1910s. Today the intersection of Hilliard Avenue and Foothill Boulevard serves as the end exit for the Glendale (2) Freeway. So much fill and earth movement has occurred that the original view is unrecognizable. Somewhere deep below the pavement of Foothill Boulevard are the beams of the trestle bridges and the original stone culverts. (Courtesy Glendale Library.)

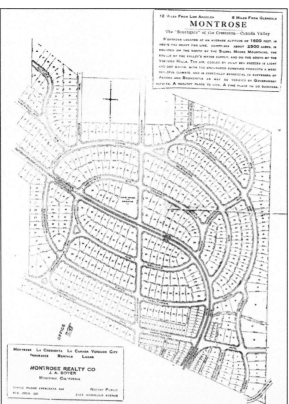

After developers Holmes and Walton bought the lower section of the valley from the Briggs family in the early 1910s, they cleared the relatively flat ground of brush and large rocks and held a contest to name the new community. Montrose (mountain rose) was chosen and the streets were laid out in the fanciful pattern of a rose. The sweeping curves of the roads still confuse newcomers.

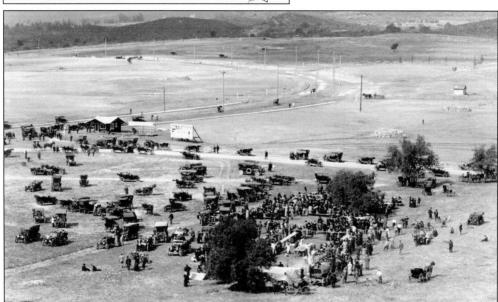

On February 22, 1913, Holmes-Walton Realtors sponsored a barbecue picnic near the intersection of Verdugo Road and Montrose Avenue, which is generally considered the "birth" of Montrose. The event was a big success, with customers spending over $60,000. However, real estate sales after that were slow, and it took years for the area to develop. In the background are the new poles along the railroad right-of-way for the coming electric trolley. (Courtesy Glendale Library.)

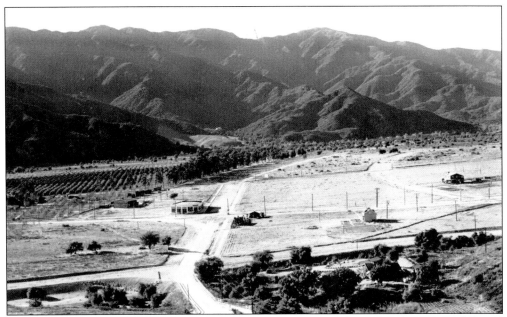

The first electric power poles were installed in La Crescenta and La Cañada in 1912, followed by eight street lights, from Rosemont Avenue to La Crescenta Avenue and south to Montrose Avenue in 1913. This 1915 photograph shows power poles in what is now downtown Montrose, as well as electric lines going up Verdugo Road toward La Cañada. Natural gas was piped to the San Fernando Valley in 1910, but lines did not reach the Crescenta Valley for another 10 years. (Courtesy Glendale Library.)

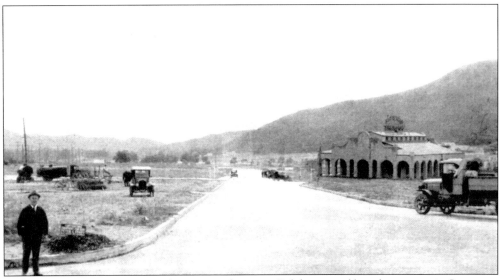

William Sparr was a pioneer in the citrus industry in California and bought acreage in Crescenta Valley just after the beginning of the 20th century. At one time, the Sparr Fruit Company was the largest in California, but in the early 1920s, Sparr subdivided the orchard and sold home lots in Sparr Heights from a lavish real estate office. He later donated the office to the community and today it survives as the Sparr Heights Community Center.

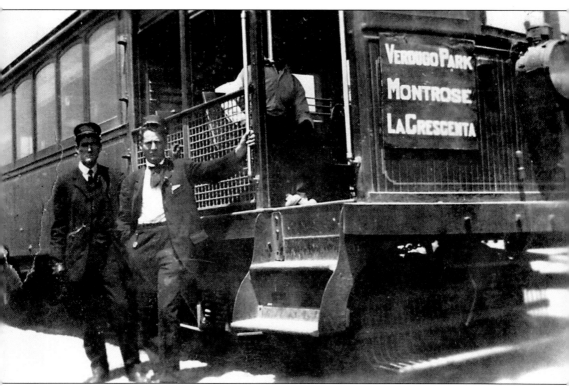

This is an electric trolley of the Glendale and Montrose Railway, which provided passenger and freight service between Los Angeles, Glendale, and the Crescenta Valley. Started in 1909 as the Glendale and Eagle Rock Railway, the tracks were extended to La Crescenta in 1913 after Walton (part of Holmes and Walton, the developers of Montrose, and the namesake of Waltonia Avenue) bought the company. He renamed it the Glendale and Montrose Railway (which holds the distinction of being the only one in Los Angeles to remain independent of the giant L.A. Railway Company or the Pacific Electric). The G&M trolley line helped fuel the huge growth spurt of the valley in the 1920s, but it went out of business in 1930, a victim of the Depression. The tracks ran up the middle of Verdugo Road and onto Montrose Avenue, which is why those streets are so wide. The line ended at Pennsylvania and the trolley cars were housed and serviced in a barn in Montrose that is now used to store lumber for Anawalt Hardware. (Photograph by Charles Shattuck; courtesy Mike Morgan.)

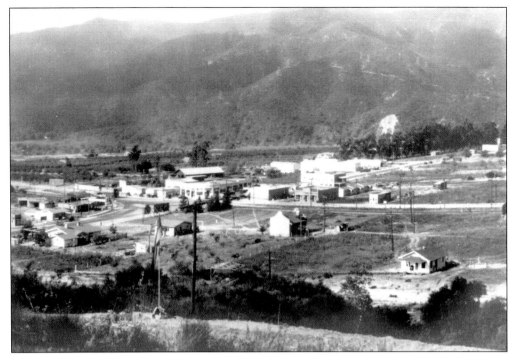

One of the first buildings constructed in the Montrose business district was the powerhouse for the Glendale and Montrose Railway. It's the small structure in the center foreground with the rounded, peaked roof. It was constructed in 1913 to house the massive generators used to electrify the trolley line to Glendale. Most of the buildings in this photograph (which was taken in the 1920s) are still in use today. (Courtesy Glendale Library.)

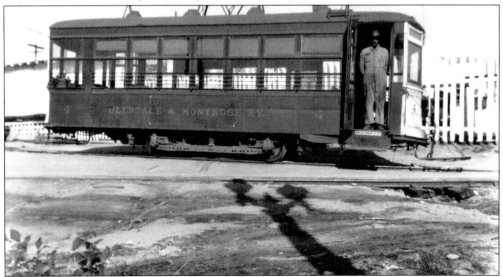

Nicknamed "The Dinky," this trolley car's single truck configuration gave it an unstable undulating motion. La Crescenta teenagers traveling to Glendale High would shift their weight in time to the rocking motion until the wheels popped off the track, derailing the car. The "bad boys" of Crescenta Valley were rewarded with an excuse for missing the first classes of the day. (Photograph by C. E. Wright; courtesy Mike Morgan.)

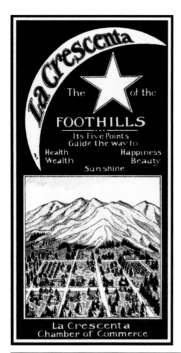

In the 1920s, the La Crescenta Chamber of Commerce put together a booklet extolling the virtues of the area, calling it the "Star of the Foothills." The chamber claimed that the star's five points "guide the way to Health, Wealth, Happiness, Beauty and Sunshine, and means much to the people of this community." (Courtesy Glendale Library.)

The sales brochure lays it on pretty thick: "You too, we hope, will agree with us and especially at a time when the icy blasts of winter howl and shriek around your home, or the sweltering heat of summer causes one extreme discomfort, you too, can avoid all this, come and be one of us . . . and avail yourself of the wonderful benefits of this glorious Land of Sunshine." (Courtesy Los Angeles Public Library.)

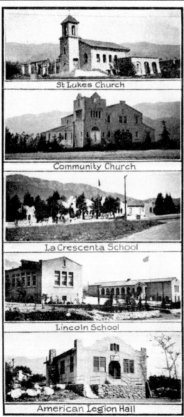

LA CRESCENTA, CALIFORNIA

Rainfall
The annual normal rainfall is about twenty-four inches a year.

Fogs
Foggy days are rare.

Health
The most healthful place on earth.

Library
Los Angeles County maintains a branch free library in La Crescenta enabling one to have free access to the wonderful literature of the county.

Radio Station KGFH
Located within our confines is a modern radio broadcasting station.

Schools
The educational facilities are constantly being increased with the growing population of La Crescenta. Two modern grade schools are maintained with an efficient staff of instructors. In the near future a $500,000 high school will be erected, the 20-acre site of which has already been purchased. In La Crescenta school in 1921 there were 81 students and three teachers.
In 1927 there were 375 students and 16 teachers at the La Crescenta school.
In the Lincoln school (completed in 1927) there are 125 students and five teachers. A total enrollment of 500 students and a staff of 21 teachers for the two schools, being an increase of 600 percent in six years. The property valuation of the two schools is $150,000.

Business and Professions
Practically all lines of business are represented by progressive dealers who carry clean, well assorted stocks. Reputable attorneys, dentists and physicians also maintain offices here.

Postal
The steady growth of La Crescenta is reflected by the increasing volume of business handled by the

Three
TOURISM AND HEALTH SEEKERS

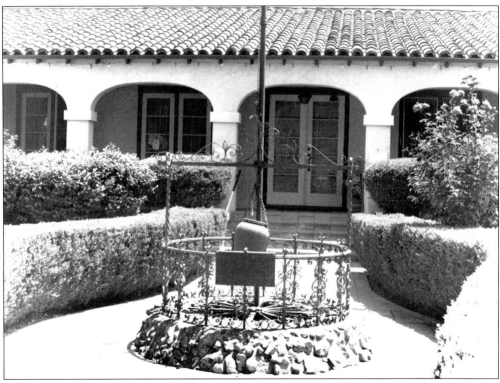

In the 1920s, this motel was built along Tujunga Canyon Road below Foothill Boulevard. The style of the motel was designed to cash in on the mission craze of that era, and the proximity to the home of Tujunga's John Steven McGroarty, author of the *Mission Play*, a popular 1920s tourist venue made this a natural spot for a legend to develop. A plaque on the faux well in the courtyard of the motel describes Rancho La Hermanos, an American Indian orphanage run by Sister Elsie, a Catholic nun. Although Sister Elsie is now a part of the fabric of local history, the Catholic church has no records of such a person. Some feel that Phil Begue used the name of Sister Else Peak (now Mount Lukens) as a starting point for this story in order to boost tourism. (Courtesy Glendale Library.)

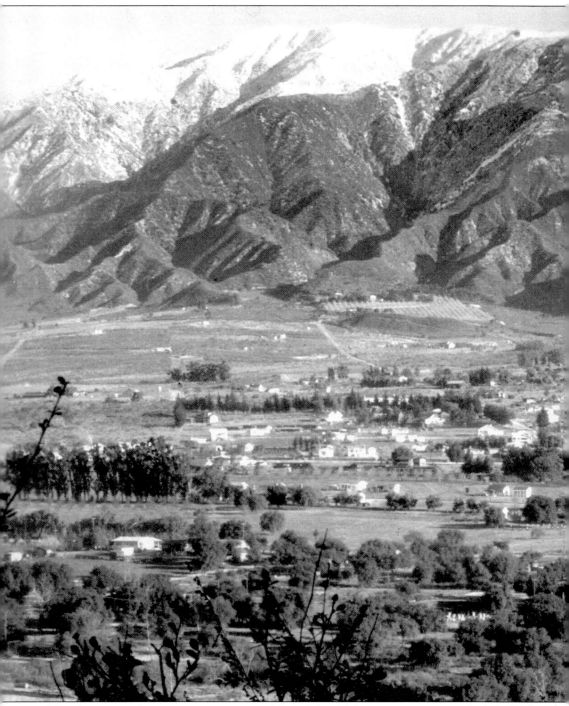

The clean air and picturesque, snowcapped San Gabriel Mountains were an early draw to the La Crescenta Valley for both tourists and those seeking a cure for asthma. Dr. Benjamin Briggs had searched the world for an ideal healthful climate and settled here, moving his family from Indiana. He built a sanitarium on Briggs Terrace to treat people with lung ailments. Many doctors followed him and the area soon became dotted with sanitariums. Ironically Briggs subdivided

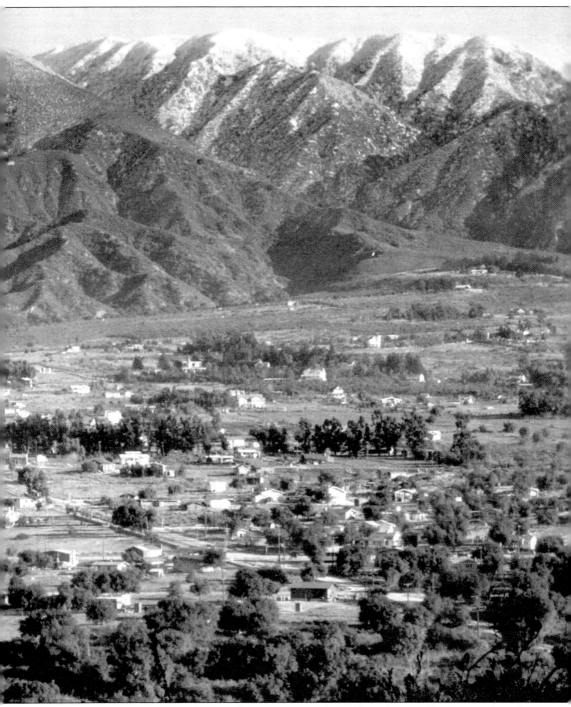

the land that he had bought and planted many trees in the valley. The population growth and those trees helped to change the microclimate of the area so that it no longer has that healthful climate. Every once in a while after a winter rain, the air is as clear as it was when this late-1910s photograph was taken. (Courtesy Glendale Library.)

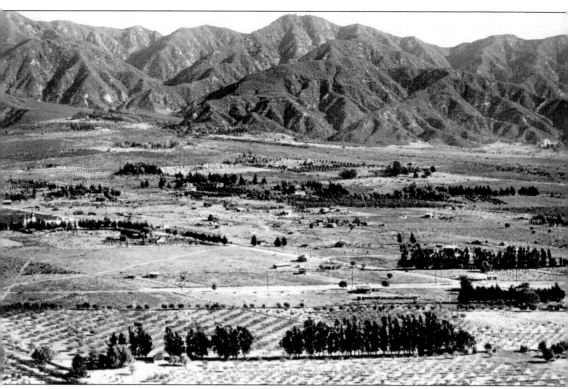

In 1890, the grand La Crescenta Hotel, also known as the Silver Tree Inn, was built among lush gardens and orchards at the intersection of Rosemont Avenue and Michigan Avenue (Foothill Boulevard), seen as the wooded area in the center of this postcard picture. The first hotel was almost immediately flattened by fierce Santa Ana winds, killing a woman who had ironically come from the Midwest to escape tornados. The hotel was immediately rebuilt, but much stronger. Operated by two delicate Southern ladies (who later owned the Fairmont), the hotel attracted an international clientele. Opera stars, artists, politicians, and religious leaders all came to breathe the healthy air and enjoy the evening entertainment in the gilded ballroom accented with red velvet and dark mahogany furniture. The valley was no longer a major tourist attraction by the mid-1920s and the hotel closed. It was turned into a boardinghouse in the 1930s and 1940s and was torn down in the 1960s to build a shopping center. (Courtesy Glendale Library.)

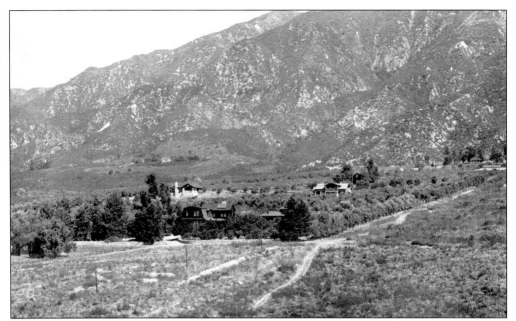

Built in 1900, the Fairmont Hotel was one of the two resort hotels in the area frequented by the well-to-do looking for clean air and a quiet retreat. The wagon track in the foreground is now Briggs Avenue. The rectangular structure on the roof of the hotel is a solar water-heating panel. The Fairmont remained a hotel for about 20 years, but was later sold and remodeled into a large home. (Courtesy Glendale Library.)

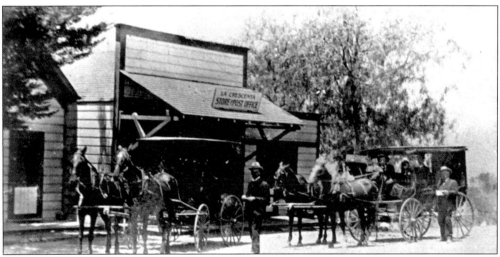

In 1895, the La Crescenta Store and Post Office at Michigan Avenue (Foothill Boulevard) and Los Angeles Street (La Crescenta Avenue) was the center of town. Also at this dusty intersection were a church, a mansion, and a five-acre park featuring a crescent-shaped fishpond and pepper trees. These two stagecoaches made regular runs to and from Pasadena, bringing guests to the resort hotels of the valley and sightseers to view Gould Castle. (Courtesy Glendale Library.)

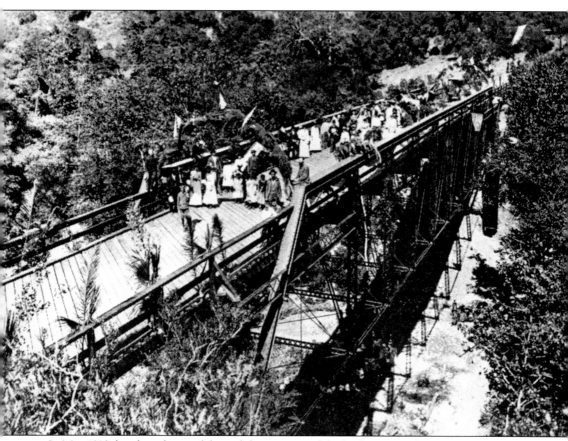

In May 1893, local residents celebrated the opening of the bridge across the Arroyo Seco at Devils Gate. This view is looking east toward Pasadena. Palm fronds, yucca blossoms, and other native vegetation were used to decorate the structure for the ceremony and community picnic. The bridge was a critical link to the tourist mecca of Pasadena for the Crescenta Valley. Tourists came in stagecoaches and cars to enjoy the air and see Gould Castle. Neighbors who lived near this bridge complained about the noise. The bridge was made of wooden planks and horse's hooves would clip-clop across, with the noise echoing in the canyon. The bridge, replaced several times since, is part of the 210 Freeway, an important link to Pasadena and points east. And neighbors still complain about the noise!

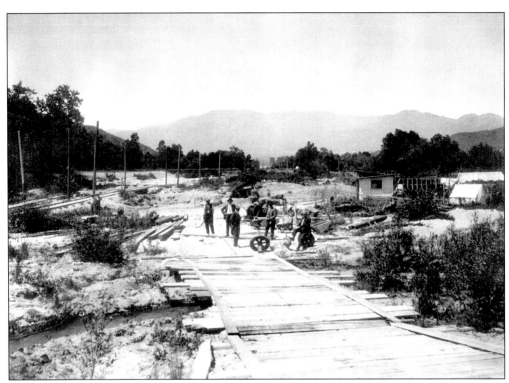

This temporary bridge across Verdugo Creek (where today's Cañada Boulevard goes over the creek near Verdugo Park) was part of a service road for the trolley. The west side of Verdugo Canyon was used for the streetcar (the tracks are visible in the background) and the east for Verdugo Road. When Walton bought the Glendale and Eagle Rock Railway in 1913, he extended it to La Crescenta to bring prospective buyers to his new community of Montrose. (Courtesy Mike Morgan.)

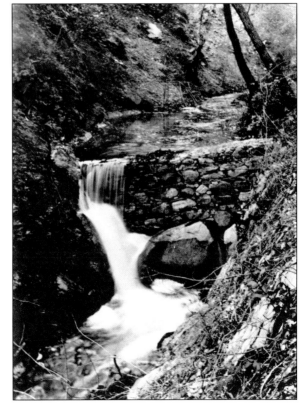

Pickens Stream was one of the few year-round watercourses that reached the valley floor. In the early 1900s, people started diverting the water higher up the canyon, siphoning it from the creek at Briggs Terrace and from the water's source deep in the mountain via horizontal water wells. As a result, Pickens Stream, now a concrete-lined channel, is bone-dry most of the year. (Courtesy Glendale Library.)

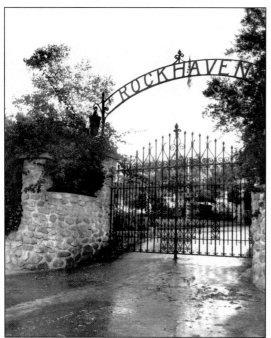

From the 1880s through World War II, there were numerous lung sanitariums in the valley, as well as others for the treatment of mental illness, such as Kimball's Sanitarium. In 1923, Agnes Richards opened Rockhaven, a facility exclusively for women, in Montrose. Over the years, the facility has treated celebrities including Billie Burke (Glenda the Good Witch in *The Wizard of Oz*), Clark Gable's wife, and Marilyn Monroe's mother. This facility is the last sanitarium in the valley. (Courtesy Glendale Library.)

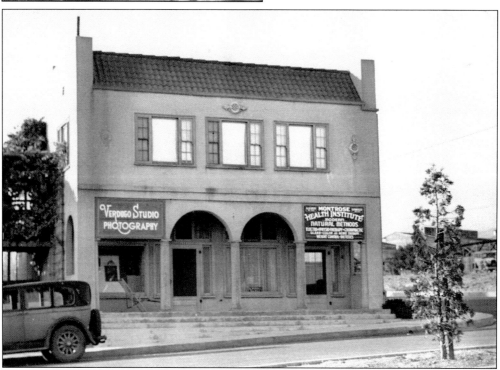

For decades, Verdugo Studios was a thriving Montrose business. Some of the photographs in this book were taken by the studio's photographers, including this one from 1936. The Montrose Health Institute on the right shows that "new age" medical treatments are not exactly new in California. Their sign proclaims "Modern Natural Methods—Electro and Physio Therapy—Chiropractic—Gland, Colon, and Nerve Therapy—Weight Control Dietetics." (Courtesy Glendale Library.)

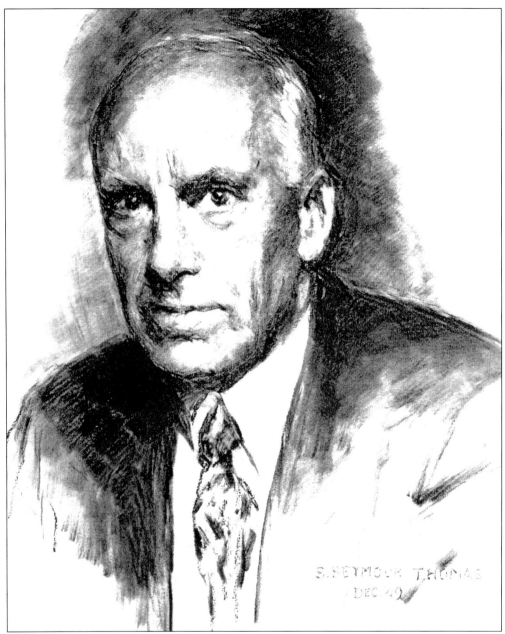

Dr. Montague Cleeves, shown here in this portrait painted by one of his patients, the famous portrait artist S. Seymour Thomas, was one of the many early residents who had been drawn to the Crescenta Valley for the health-giving properties of its air. In the 1920s, Cleeves emigrated from northern England where he witnessed the plight of coal miners and their terrible lung problems. He obtained a California medical degree and encouraged others to take advantage of the air in La Crescenta. He carved out a beautiful home and garden in a section of his 20 acres near the top of Briggs. In front of his home, he posted a sign that read, "Sunnyslope: A Place In The Sun Reserved For Children." He doted on his own children and, with his wife, was very involved in the community. One of his daughters became a leading female scientist. Dr. Marian Diamond is a professor of anatomy at Berkeley. (Courtesy Dr. Marian Diamond.)

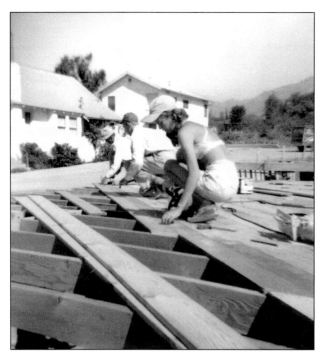

In 1949, Glen Hine nails down the subfloor on a future Crescenta Valley fixture—the May Lane Motel, named for his son Maynard ("May") and his daughter Alane ("Lane"), seen here helping. At the age of 13, Hine had moved from job to job, working at the Indianapolis Raceway, as a cowboy, prospector, an airplane mechanic, and painter. He ran the motel until his death in 1964. (Courtesy Maynard Hine.)

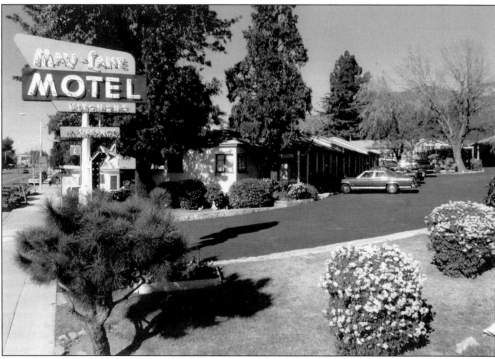

For almost half a century, the May Lane Motel was the "extra bedroom of CV." Many longtime residents have put visiting relatives and friends up at the May Lane. The motel was also used in film and television productions, including *Radio Flyer* and *The X-Files*. No longer named the May Lane, the La Crescenta Motel lives on borrowed time, as developers plan to tear it down soon. (Courtesy Maynard Hine.)

Four

SHACKS AND CASTLES

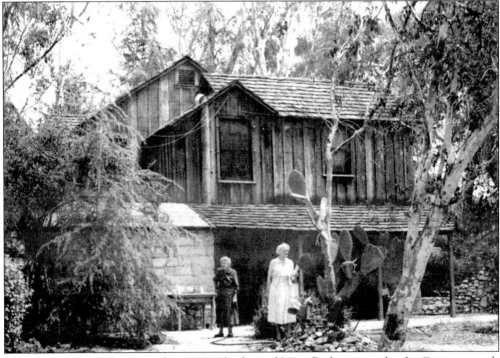

Claiming a 160-acre homestead in 1886, Charles and Mary Bathey arrived in La Crescenta with their children Winifred, Allie, Edith, and Herbert. They built this mountain cabin near Briggs Terrace. It has survived fires, floods, wind, and the pressures of development for over 100 years. Ironically Charles Bathey supervised the construction of one of the two castles built in the area—Gould Castle. He lived in a cabin while he built the castle. Winifred Bathey and Ellie Johnson, right, stayed in the family home until its sale in the 1960s. The grounds are heavily overgrown and the cabin is difficult to see from the street, but locals say it still looks like this. (Courtesy La Crescenta Library.)

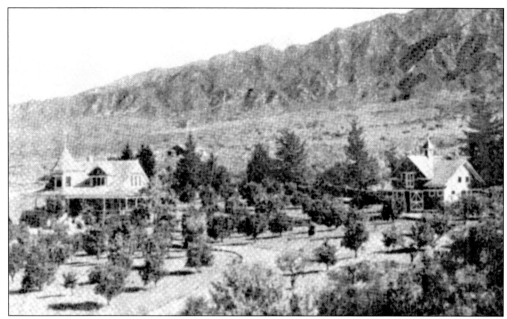

Shot around 1910, this photograph shows the Victorian mansion and grounds of the Czerniski estate. The house, purchased by Merritt Kimball in 1923, was occupied by the Kimball family, as well as staff, and run as the Kimball Sanitarium. Historians estimate that the house was built in the 1880s and stood for 80 years before being torn down to make room for the La Crescenta Shopping Center.

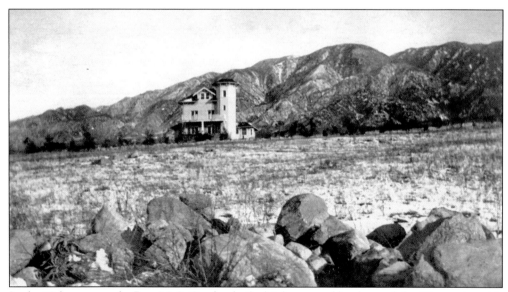

In the 19th century, the Rev. M. S. Gordon built this house and landscaped the 10-acre site with orange, palm, olive, pomegranate, cedar trees, and a vineyard. In 1910, James Basil McLaughlin took ownership of it as a settlement for attorney's fees. Laughlin Street was named in his honor, with the "Mc" being dropped immediately. The home was a local landmark until the 1971 Sylmar earthquake undermined it so badly that it had to be demolished. (Courtesy Glendale Library.)

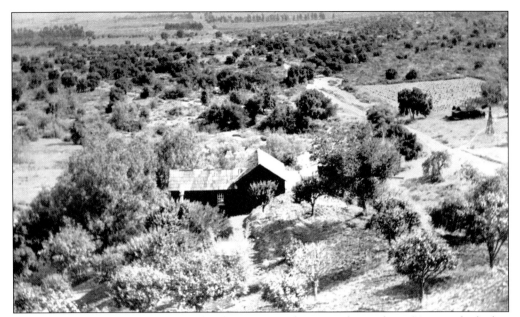

This was the cabin of George Englehardt, a German homesteader in the 1870s, as it looked in 1912 when Col. Homer Baldridge of Pasadena bought it and the surrounding 138 acres. Famed opera star Lawrence Tibbitt lived in the cabin when he worked for the colonel in the orchards, singing while he worked. This site now overlooks Oakmont Woods and the wagon track on the right is La Crescenta Avenue.

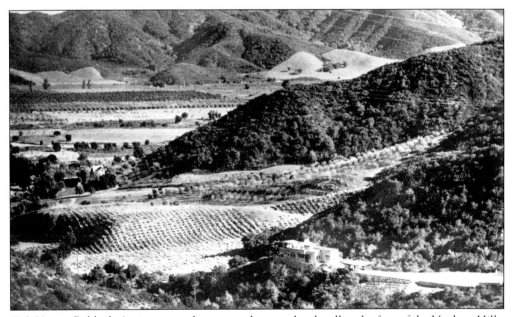

Col. Homer Baldridge's picturesque home stands atop a low knoll at the foot of the Verdugo Hills. The house was named "Onondarka," an American Indian word meaning "House on the Hill." Onondarka Ranch, the setting for hayrides, was also the scene of rodeos after World War II. The ranch was sold and subdivided in the late 1940s and developed into housing tracts, but the "House on the Hill" remains in the area now known as Oakmont Woods. (Courtesy Katherine Halford.)

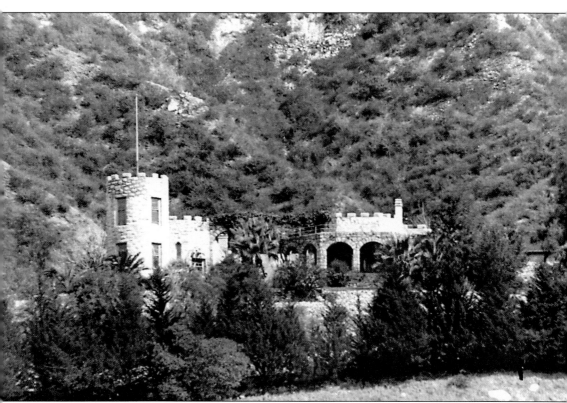

In the late 1880s, "raisin king" Eugene H. Gould purchased 185 acres high on the slopes of the valley just east of Pickens Canyon as a site for his winter home. His artistically talented wife, May I. Gould, a niece of Dr. Benjamin Briggs, sketched drawings of a castle she had seen in Spain and, thanks to her husband's wealth, had the castle built to her specifications. In 1892, construction was completed. The castle was laid out with the living quarters separated from the sleeping quarters by a large outdoor patio with huge arches. The western wing contained the bedrooms and a tall tower that housed Mrs. Gould's art studio. The eastern wing contained a great room with marble pillars and large arched windows. Also in this wing were the dining hall, servant's quarters, and kitchen cellars. A wide veranda that ran along the front of the house offered spectacular views of the valley. The huge structure and lavish furnishings were a draw for tourists and the Goulds held many sumptuous parties there. (Courtesy Lanterman.)

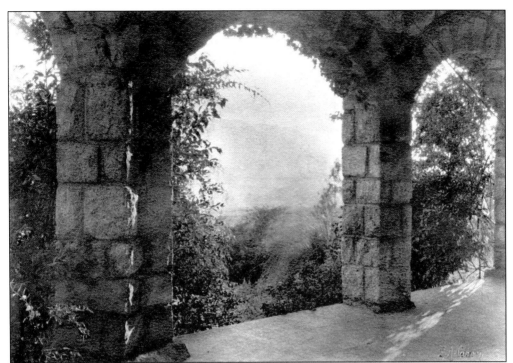

Charles T. Bathey supervised the building of the Gould castle. The walls were constructed of granite quarried from spots all over the Crescenta Valley floor where they had been deposited by past floods (like the large boulders that were strewn across the valley after the great flood of 1934). Crews searched for these giant boulders and notified Bathey. (Courtesy Glendale Library.)

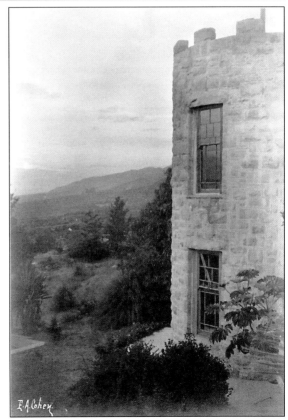

When workers found a boulder that Bathey thought was acceptable, they drilled holes into the rock and then hammered wedges into the holes, splitting the boulders into manageable sizes. As recently as the 1940s, people claimed to find rock chips and fragments left behind. Bathey had built a horse-powered cable car to haul the stones from the valley floor up to the building site. A former Royal British Navy officer named Elliot cut all the granite blocks. (Courtesy Glendale Library.)

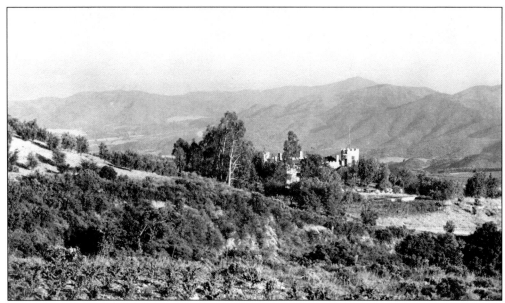

At some point in the late 1890s and early 1900s, Eugene Gold tried to corner the raisin market. He failed miserably and was forced to sell all his properties to pay his debts. The Goulds moved out of the castle and into the caretaker's cottage in a futile attempt to keep possession. Castles are hard to maintain, however, and only a few people lived in it before it was torn down in 1955. (Courtesy Glendale Library.)

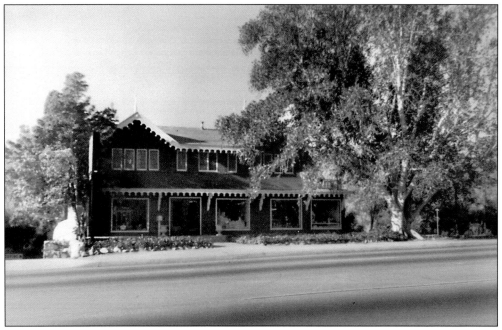

This house, along with its huge Morton Bay fig tree, is a landmark on Foothill Boulevard near Rosemont Avenue. The Colonial-style house was built in 1915 for Helen Eaton. The grounds included olive groves behind the house, the survivors of which are still a feature of Mary Street, one block away. The fig tree is thought to be a descendent of the "silver tree" of the Silver Tree Inn (later the La Crescenta Hotel) across the street.

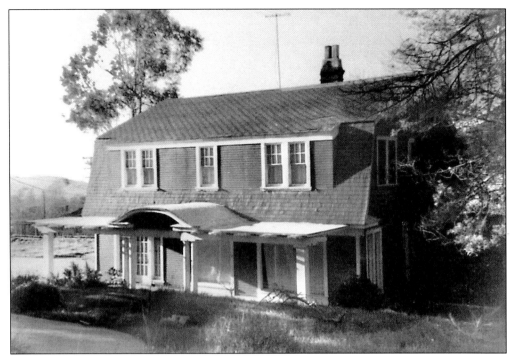

This charming, barn-style house built in the 1920s was on the corner of Rosemont Avenue and Foothill Boulevard. The Atwaters lived there in the 1940s, when Mr. Atwater died in a car crash, followed shortly by his wife and daughter, also in car crashes, leaving Buddy Atwater the sole survivor of the family. The home, an antique store in the 1980s, was demolished in 2001 and an office building erected in its place.

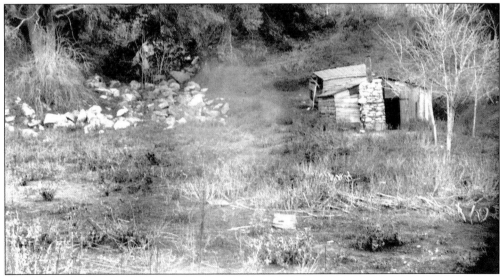

During the Depression, when "Okies" moved west to escape the dust bowl, many poor people moved into the canyons above La Crescenta, living in tents and shacks like this one in Pickens Canyon. The official death toll of the 1934 flood did not include these squatters, which inspired Woody Guthrie to record "The Los Angeles New Year's Flood," singing of the Okies who drowned with no one knowing or caring about their fate. (Courtesy Glendale Library.)

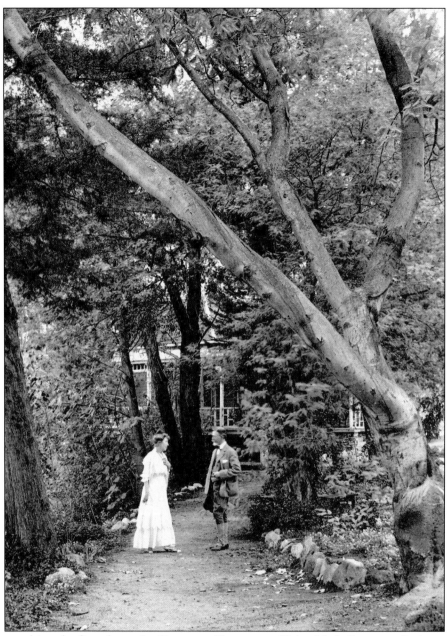

After teaching the first class at La Crescenta Elementary, Helen Haskell went to Paris to study art. She fell in love with and married promising young American artist S. Seymour Thomas, who became one of the most famous portrait artists in the United States. After the start of World War I, Helen inherited acreage on Briggs Terrace from her aunt and the couple decided to settle down in the Crescenta Valley. They bought an old and heavily wooded property just above the La Crescenta Hotel at Rosemont Avenue and Foothill Boulevard, which had a rambling, old home and a stone outbuilding that served as an artist's studio. Their comfortable home, known as "Cuddle Doone," was named after a Scottish poem and expression that roughly means "cuddled down in bed." The Thomases were heavily involved in the community and Seymour painted what became the plan for St. Luke's Church. (Courtesy Witte Museum.)

In this photograph from the 1920s, Helen Haskell Thomas and her servant prepare the sumptuously decorated Thomas home to receive visitors for a Sunday afternoon tea and reception to view Seymour Thomas's latest works. These teas were part social event and part business, since the rich and famous of that era were attracted by the hundreds to the Thomas home and often commissioned portraits as a result. (Courtesy Witte Museum.)

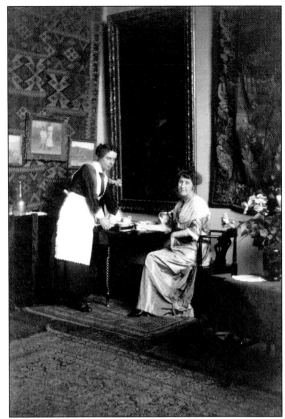

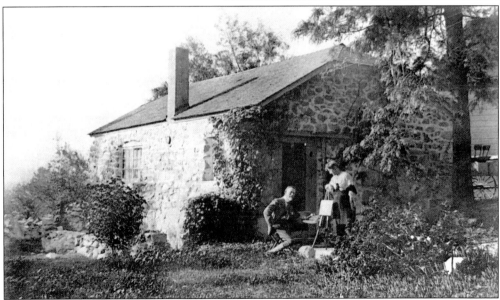

Seymour Thomas liked to paint small landscapes outside his studio at "Cuddle Doone" or in the surrounding countryside as a means of relaxation between portraits. He often gave these landscape paintings away as gifts, some signed informally, some not at all, which causes confusion in today's art market as Thomas's work becomes more valuable. (Courtesy Witte Museum.)

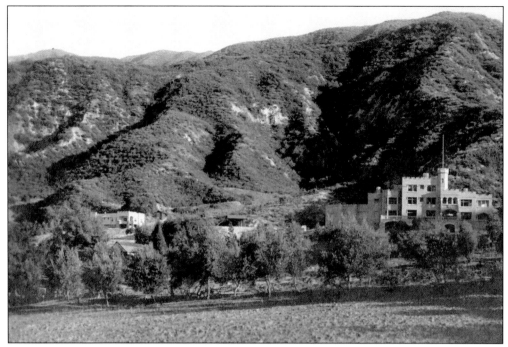

In 1911, Albert Wallace, California's lieutenant governor, built another castle near Gould Castle, but Wallace's wife felt that pre-Flintridge La Cañada was not up to her social standards so they sold it in 1914. Frank Strong moved in with his new bride, but almost immediately took off carousing. To anger him, Strong's young wife had the castle painted bright pink, and the castle remained that color for the next 70 years.

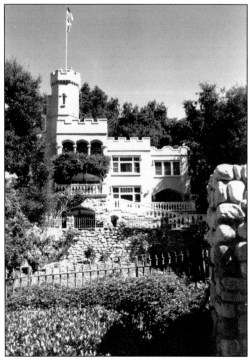

In the 1950s, the "Pink Castle" was sold to developers, who subdivided the 75-acre estate and left the castle abandoned. It was looted and left open to partying teenagers. In the late 1960s, it was reinhabited and in 1990, it was painted light gray. Since 1992, the owners, George and Annsley Strong (no relation to early owner Frank Strong), have completed the restoration to its original 1911 grandeur.

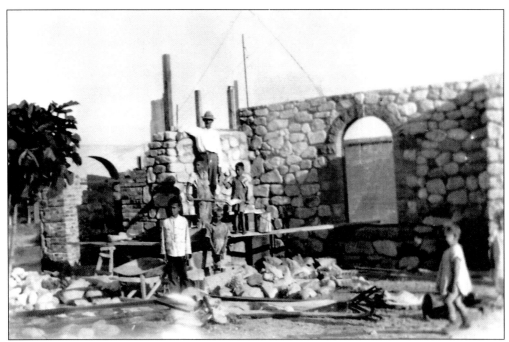

Julius Rakasits bought a plot of land on Cross Street, where, with the help of his family, he built a house out of stone that took 20 years to complete. In this late 1920s photograph, Rakasits and his kids are working on the house. They hauled much of the stone from Tujunga Canyon because Rakasits felt that the stone there was "cleaner"—true rounded river rock. The house still stands. (Courtesy Joe and Linda Rakasits.)

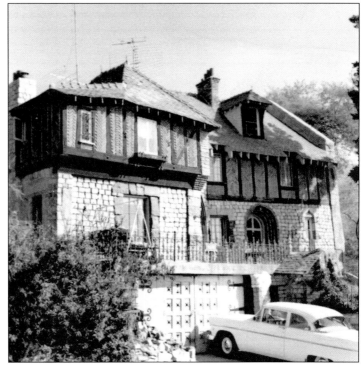

Owners and restorers of this unusual home on Briggs Terrace, the Berg family was told that it was constructed from old movie props. Initially built in 1910, the house was later enlarged by Paramount executive Edward Jeanette. Parts of the house were from the sets of *Robin Hood* and *Ben Hur*. Some of the interior accents once belonged to Edward G. Robinson, Randolph Hearst, and the "It" girl, Clara Bow. (Courtesy Glendale Library.)

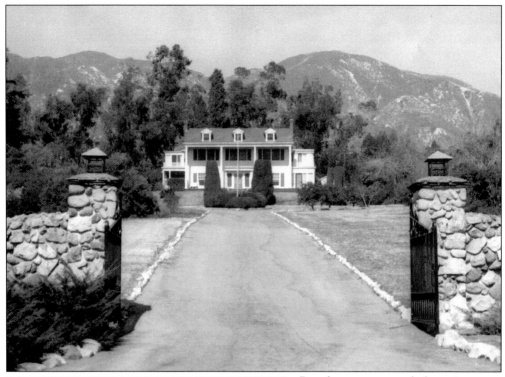

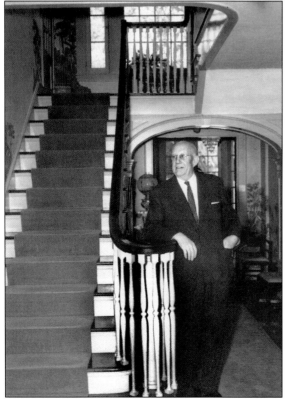

Based on an ancestral plantation, this magnificent mansion was built by Thomas C. Thornton, but was later known as the Bishop Estate. Construction started in 1917 and wasn't completed until 1923. Because of the regular gale force winds of the valley, steel cables were anchored in the ground and attached to the roof beams, literally holding down the house. The cables, though, couldn't prevent the City of Glendale from tearing it down in 1966 to build Mountain Avenue School. (Courtesy Glendale Library.)

The Bishop Estate featured a sweeping mahogany staircase rising to a stained glass window at the landing, with eight bedrooms upstairs, all with fireplaces and hardwood floors. Locals say that when the mansion was torn down, the staircase was disassembled and reinstalled in one of the homes nearby. Does this staircase look familiar to anyone? (Courtesy Glendale Library.)

Five

DAILY LIFE

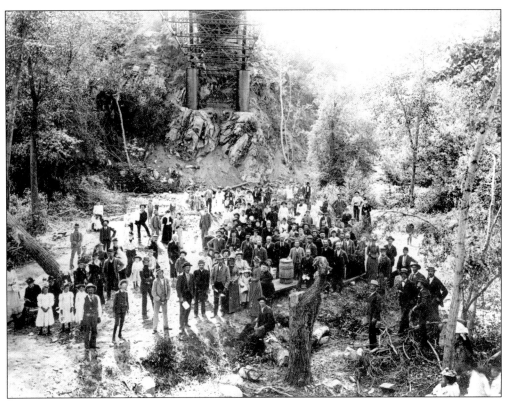

As La Crescenta grew, it gradually took on the trappings of a real community. Schools and churches were built. Businesses opened (and closed). More roads were paved, and train and bus lines carried people to and from the area. As people sought relaxation in the form of parks and outdoor activities, picnics became a regular part of the social fabric of the valley, and the blazing heat of summer in the pre-air-conditioned, scrub-covered Crescenta Valley often sent residents to seek the shade of the tree-lined canyons. In this 1890s photograph, picnickers are enjoying the natural coolness of the Arroyo at Devil's Gate under the bridge to Pasadena, with the center of attention being a big barrel of liquid refreshment. (Courtesy Glendale Library.)

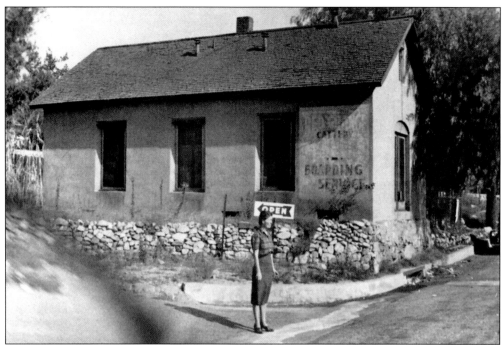

Dr. Benjamin Briggs donated the grounds for the first school, which was erected in 1886 of solid concrete and stone on the corner of Foothill and Dyer. Briggs convinced his niece Helen Haskell to teach the first classes, and records show that 19 students enrolled that year. La Crescenta Presbyterian Church later occupied this building until 1923. It then fell into a variety of uses with the last being a real estate office in the 1950s. (Courtesy Glendale Library.)

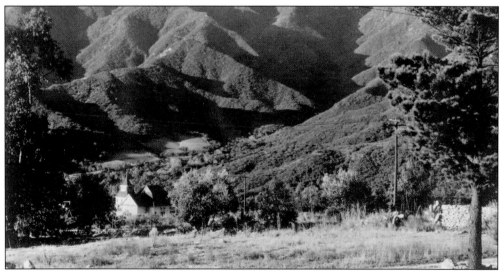

Because of the growing population of the valley, the school was almost immediately outgrown and in 1890, a son-in-law of Dr. Briggs donated land on which this simple, steepled one-room schoolhouse was built. La Crescenta School opened that year with 29 students. The bell in the steeple, able to be heard throughout the valley, rang the kids to school each morning. The bell still exists on the same grounds where newer La Crescenta Elementary now stands. (Courtesy Glendale Library.)

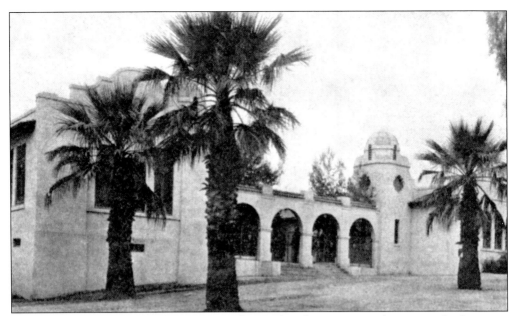

This Mediterranean-style building was erected in 1915 on the same site as the previous La Crescenta School, when La Crescenta Avenue was still unpaved and known as Los Angeles Street. This 1916 photograph shows the central patio and tall tower, which housed the school bell.

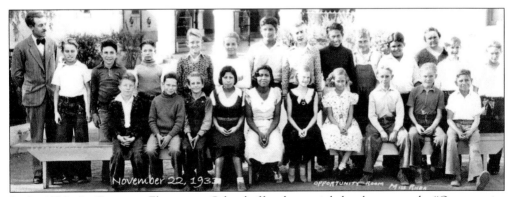

In the 1930s, La Crescenta Elementary School offered a special class known as the "Opportunity Room." Taught by Miss Ray (back row, far right), the Opportunity Room was for students who were having problems either socially or academically; they were given the "opportunity" to do better. This class was also for children who had limited English skills. Principal Bert Steelhead stands to the left. (Courtesy Dorothy Hubert.)

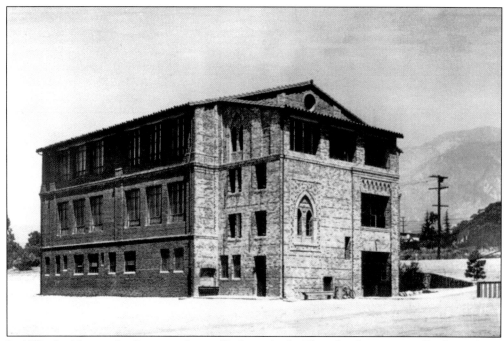

In 1932, the 10-room La Crescenta Junior High was built. The school was originally planned as a high school, but with the La Crescenta and Glendale School Districts merger in 1931, valley high school students instead attended Glendale High. This building still exists, but it's been added on to so many times it's hard to recognize. (Courtesy Glendale School District.)

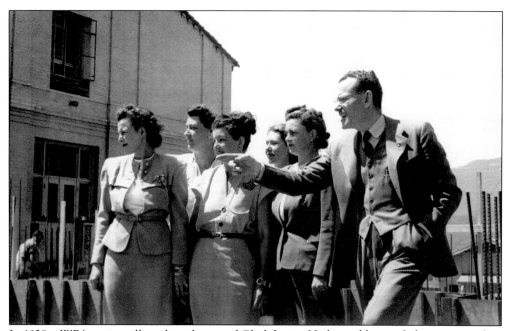

In 1938, a WPA project allowed newly named Clark Junior High to add several classrooms and an auditorium. Here the principal shows school board members the progress on the construction of the new building on the west side of the original structure. (Courtesy Glendale School District.)

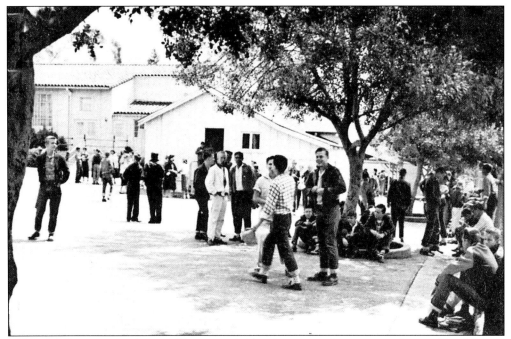

Life at Clark Junior High in 1955 was much like the movie *Grease*, according to Floyd Farrar, wearing the plaid shirt in the center of this photograph. "We always talked about cool cars. James Dean and *Rebel Without A Cause* was the best movie ever to us." Rolled-up Levis and PF Flyers were standard for boys, but the cool shoes were blue suede or penny loafers. And you really did put a penny in them. (Courtesy Floyd Farrar.)

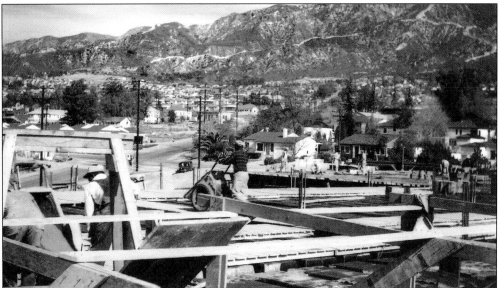

In 1955, the booming population of the valley was demanding its own high school. Work began on a huge new three-story building on the campus of Clark Junior High. This building would, besides adding scores of new classrooms, be the new entrance to the school. In 1961, the enlarged Clark was renamed Crescenta Valley High School and the Clark name moved to the new junior high on New York Avenue. (Courtesy Vic Pallos.)

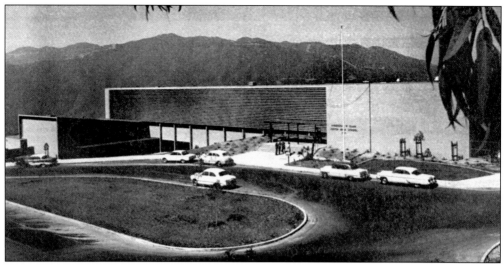

The name of Anderson W. Clark has been given to three different schools in the valley. La Crescenta Junior High School was renamed Anderson W. Clark Junior High School in 1938 after his death. Clark Junior High became Crescenta Valley High School in 1961, and a new Clark Junior High was built above Foothill Boulevard (shown here in 1962). Clark Junior High closed in 1982, but reopened in 1998 as Anderson W. Clark Magnet High School. (Courtesy Glendale School District.)

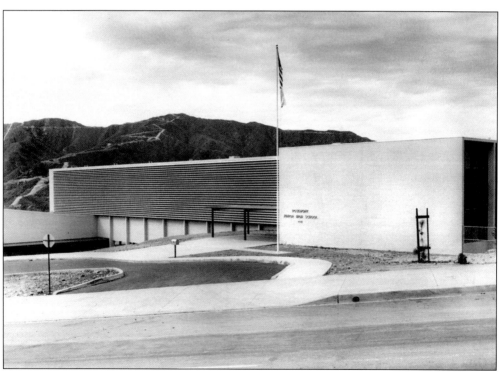

At the peak of the baby boom, the district had to add even more schools. They built Rosemont Junior High School (shown here) at 4725 Rosemont Avenue and used the same general design to build a nearly identical Clark Junior High School on New York Avenue. People still get confused by the similarities of the buildings.

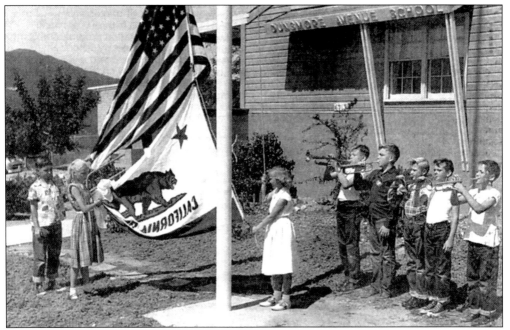

Dunsmore Elementary School opened just after World War II. In 1947, wooden barracks from an army base in Santa Ana were moved to a patch of weeds on Dunsmore Avenue and remodeled into classrooms. In 1951, the campus was further expanded with bungalows borrowed from Lincoln Elementary. Although the school has been remodeled over the years, the original barracks shape is still recognizable in the main buildings. (Courtesy La Crescenta Library.)

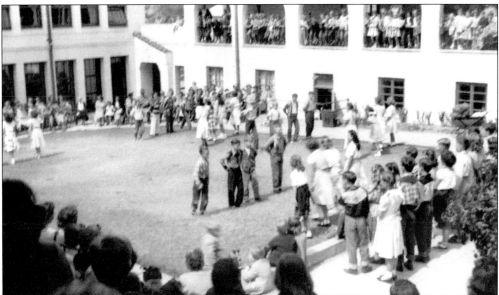

On a winter night in the 1930s, an aviator low on gas and lost in thick fog over Crescenta Valley, spotted the streetlights of Honolulu Avenue. He somehow landed on the wide street without hitting any wires and spent the night in his plane. When the fog cleared the next day, early Montrose Elementary School students (pictured here at another date) walked a block down to Honolulu Avenue to watch him take off. (Courtesy Glendale School District.)

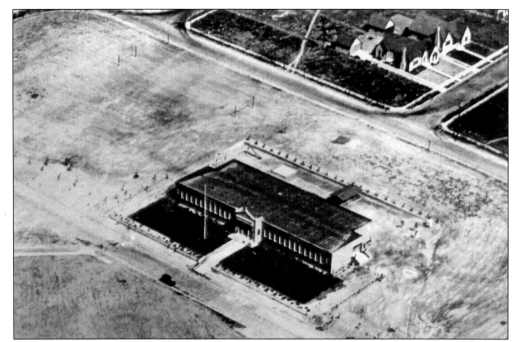

This was the new John C. Fremont Elementary School in 1928. The Sparr Realty Company began selling homes a few years earlier in Oakmont Park, now called Sparr Heights. The homes were very expensive for those times, ranging from $15,000 to $40,000. The intersection of Arlington and Rosemary Avenues can be seen behind the school. (Courtesy Vic Pallos.)

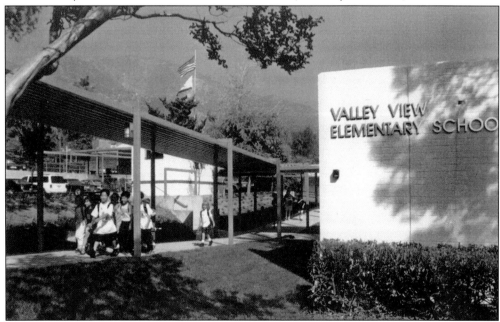

Valley View Elementary School, originally built in 1958 high above Foothill Boulevard, overlooked the valley, as its name suggests. A victim of the school district enrollment drops of the 1980s, it closed but was retained by the GUSD and leased to a private Armenian school. In 1998, it was reopened as a public school. (Courtesy Glendale School District.)

In 1927, the Watchorn Chimes were installed in the bell tower of St. Luke's, a gift of the Watchorn family in memory of their son who had perished in World War I. The chimes are rung by a set of ancient electric solenoids imported from Europe and a dedicated group of volunteers today maintains this quirky and antiquated machinery so that the beautiful tones of the chimes still ring hourly across the valley. (Courtesy Katherine Halford.)

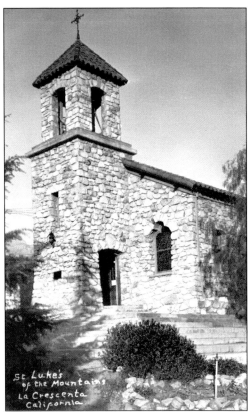

Many of the churches of La Crescenta have clustered along Montrose Avenue. Unity Church of the Valley at 2817 Montrose started in 1937, meeting in the La Crescenta Women's Club until the parishioners built this church building in 1955. Membership grew to 250, with an added 250 children in their Sunday school. But changing demographics of the valley have resulted in declining membership. Unity Church now shares its chapel with four other area churches. (Courtesy Unity Church.)

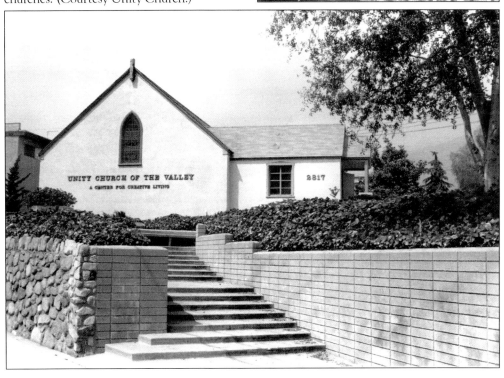

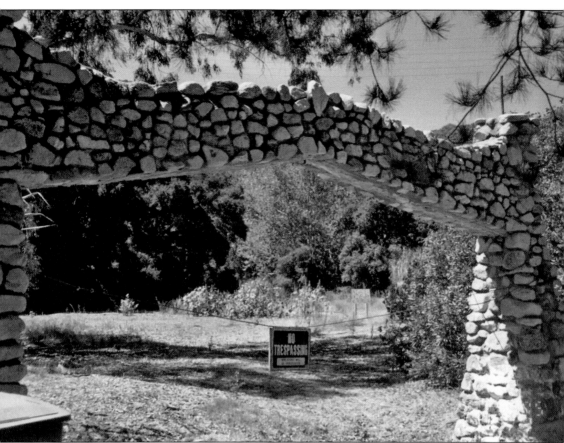

This stone archway, still standing at the bottom of New York Avenue, once welcomed guests to the Mountain Oaks Resort. In 1929, Emmit and Helen Kadlitz bought the 33-acre site. The main building had been a speakeasy, gambling hall, and the scene of many wild parties. The Kadlitzes came up with an unusual business plan by carving up 20 of the acres into 400 tiny (about 10 feet by 10 feet) tent lots. Buying one of the lots gave the owner use of the facilities. The Kadlitzes built an impressive array of attractions, including a large swimming pool, trout ponds, ball fields, picnic facilities, stables, horse trails, and turned the already existing two-story main building into a lodge with a large dance floor. However, the depression put the squeeze on the project and it never was fully realized. Company picnics, school outings, school proms, and opening the Crystal Pool for public admission kept the Kadlitz family going. The resort declined and by the 1960s was virtually abandoned. The patchwork nature of the land ownership due to the tent-lot scheme has kept the area undeveloped.

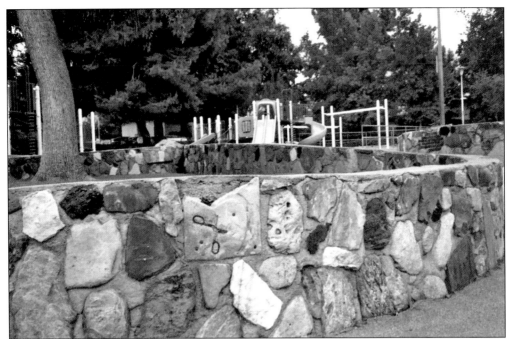

In 1946, Milton Hofert bought Dunsmore Sanitarium. He was an avid rock and junk collector. Using these materials, Hofert constructed hundreds of yards of whimsical and decorative walls on the property. In 1956, Glendale wished to create a park out of the site. Hofert negotiated a lower price with the city in exchange for an agreement to preserve his creations. Dunsmore Park today still contains most of those hodgepodge walls.

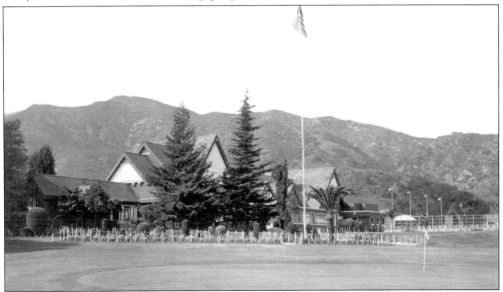

The Oakmont Country Club started in 1922 as a nine-hole course built on the grounds of a grape vineyard by local developers W. S. Sparr and F. P. Newport. A year later, members pitched in to expand the course, spending their weekends digging up and hauling out rocks, tree stumps, and grapevines. In the early days, the wash running through the grounds was full of sand and gravel and golfers had to play through the debris. (Courtesy Katherine Halford.)

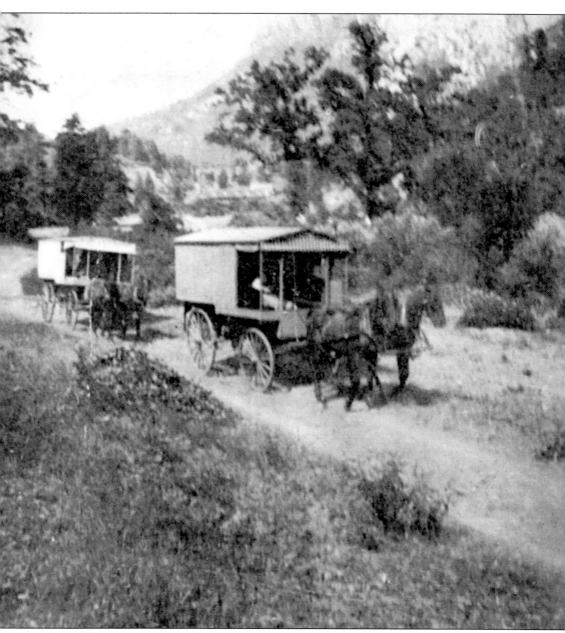

One of the great attractions of the Crescenta Valley is the San Gabriel Mountains above it. Most residents are enthusiastic outdoors people. Even early on, residents of the area enjoyed the great outdoors. In this late 1890s photograph, the Henry Slutman and Edgar Peet families—La Cañada residents—took a vacation driving their horse-drawn campers all the way to Oregon. They toured through the rugged areas of California, fishing, hunting, and panning for gold on the way. Is that an Adventure Pass hanging from the awning of the rear camper?

Hiking has always been popular in the area, even at the turn of the 19th century when groups of young people followed a maze of trails into the San Gabriels from trailheads in La Crescenta. Modern trail builders often find they have no need to construct new trails. They merely clear the brush from the scores of century-old trails that crisscross the mountains above La Crescenta. (Courtesy Don and Esther Norbut.)

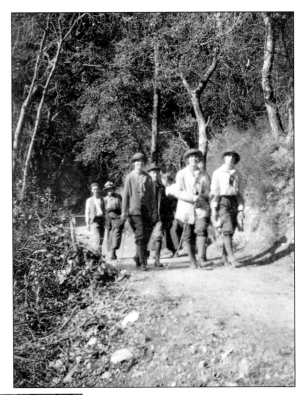

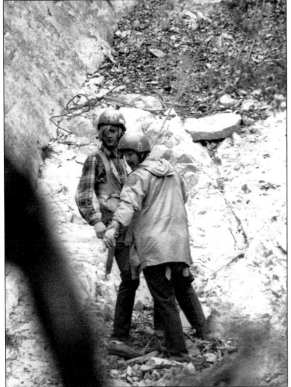

In 1976, the Montrose Search and Rescue Team (SAR) participate in a ropes training course. The group has its roots in the local Air Raid Warden group from World War II. One of the first and best SAR teams in the country, they have flown around the world to aid in rescues and train other groups. They are made up of volunteers from the community and are deputized under the authority of the Los Angeles County Sheriff. (Courtesy Glendale Library.)

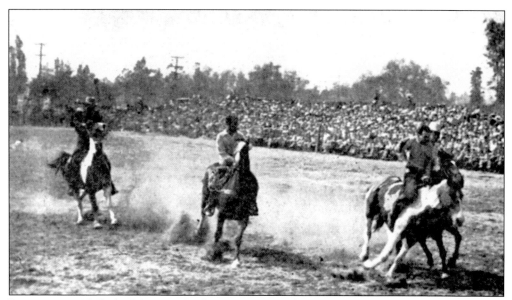

Beginning in 1945, the Montrose Rodeo was an annual event staged at the Onondarka Ranch. Visitors came from all over the Los Angeles area to watch the cowboys perform. This 1946 photograph shows a bareback riding event as "pick-up riders" try to stop a runaway paint horse. The rodeos stopped about the time the Onondarka Ranch was sold. (Courtesy Jean Maluccio.)

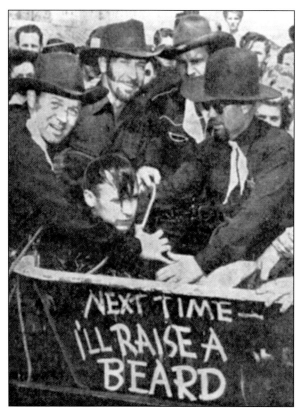

The Montrose business district took advantage of the tourists coming to the area for the rodeo by decorating the area with Western themes. The stores offered "rodeo specials" and some dressed in cowboy-style garb. One of the publicity stunts was a "No Shaving" edict during which the men were not allowed to shave. Here businessman Roger Thompson was dunked in a tub of cold water as his penalty for shaving. (Courtesy Jean Maluccio.)

After her win in the 1948 Olympics, Crescenta Valley swim star Vicki Manalo Draves used her fame to attract students to the Draves' swimming school and pool at Indian Springs. They put on many elaborate swimming shows at the local pool and went on international show tours with Buster Crabbe and others, often taking young La Crescenta swimmers with them.

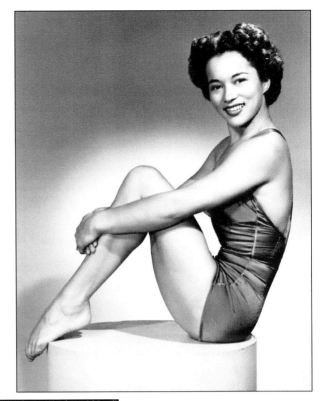

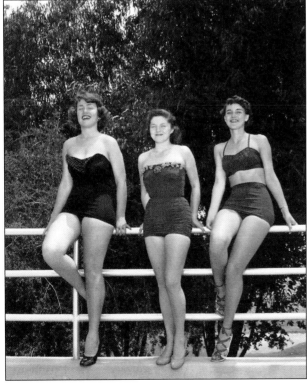

Three contestants pose for the Days of Verdugo beauty contest. Almost every event in the Crescenta Valley used a beauty contest of some sort for promotional purposes and *The Ledger* printed the photograph of a beautiful woman on the front page of virtually every edition.

STAGES   STAGES

Round trip, La Crescenta to Little Landers, 30c.
Round Trip to Sunland and Monte Vista, 40c.

VIA GLENDALE & MONTROSE RY.

TIME SCHEDULE

	*	*	*	*	*	*	*	*	xx
Lv. Los Angeles, P. E. Ry.	6:05	7:45	8:45	10:45	1:45	2:45	3:45	4:45	11:00
Lv. Glendale, G. & M. Ry.	6:35	8:20	9:20	11:20	2:20	3:20	4:20	5:20	11:40
Lv. La Crescenta, Val. Stage	7:05	8:45	9:45	11:45	2:45	3:45	4:45	5:45	12:10
Ar. Little Landers	7:35	9:15	10:15	12:15	3:15	4:15	5:15	6:15	12:40
Ar. Sunland	7:45			12:25		4:25		6:25	12:50

	*	*	*	*	*	*	*	*	xx
Lv. Sunland, Valley Stage	7:10	8:10			1:10		4:35		10:15
Lv. Little Landers, Valley Stage	7:20	8:20	9:20	10:20	1:20	3:20	4:50	5:20	10:30
Lv. La Crescenta, G. & M. Ry.	7:50	8:50	9:50	10:50	1:50	3:50	5:20	5:50	11:00
Lv. Glendale, P. E. Ry.	8:20	9:15	10:15	11:15	2:15	4:15	5:45	6:15	11:30
Ar. Los Angeles	8:55	9:55	10:55	11:55	2:55	4:55	6:25	6:55	11:55

*Daily. Light figures A. M. Dark figures P. M.
xxTheater Special. Saturdays only. One-way fare on this run 15 cents between La Crescenta and Lowell Ave.; Little Landers, 30 cents; Sunland, 35 cents.

VALLEY STAGE COMPANY

LOS ANGELES AVE.   LA CRESCENTA.

Bus service (called stages) linked Los Angeles with the Crescenta Valley starting just after World War I. Connections at the end of the line for the Glendale and Montrose Railway at Pennsylvania and Montrose Avenue were also established. In 1918, six 14-passenger Studebaker buses trundled between Sunland and Los Angeles, a two-hour trip time. When the trolley was discontinued in 1930, the Pacific Electric put their modern fleet of buses in service. (Courtesy Mike Morgan.)

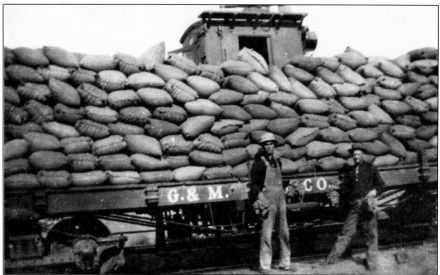

The Glendale and Montrose Railway, besides its passenger service, ran a lucrative freight business to and from the Crescenta Valley. There was a loading dock at the railhead at Montrose and Los Angeles Street (La Crescenta Avenue) and wagons from all over the valley and Sunland-Tujunga would bring grapes, olives, fruit, gravel, and silica here to be transported to Los Angeles on the electric railway. (Photograph by Charles Shattuck; courtesy Mike Morgan.)

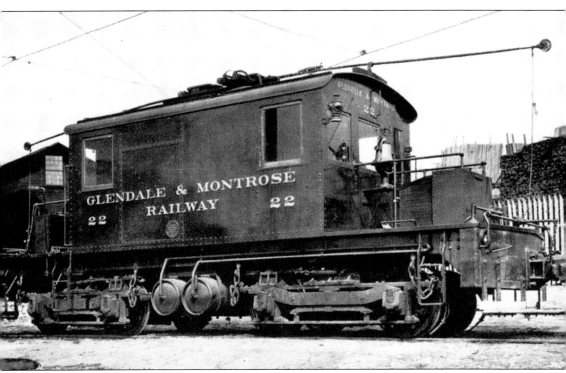

The Glendale and Montrose Railway's powerful electric locomotive pulled freight cars back and forth from Glendale throughout the 1920s. In 1923, the locomotive was stopped on a siding at Verdugo Park when an unattended freight locomotive accidentally began rolling down the tracks toward Glendale. Workmen gave chase using this electric locomotive. The runaway train picked up speed fast, careening down Glendale Avenue at 30 miles per hour, but the locomotive caught up with it and a daring man leaped onto the unmanned car. He tried to get to the brakes, but the runaway car slammed into a steam locomotive, killing the brave man. This locomotive stayed in service in Glendale until 1936, when it was sold to Yakima Valley in Washington to haul apples. It served reliably until 1985, when it was donated to the Orange Empire Railway Museum in Perris, California, where it is still run regularly. The faint impressions of the words "Glendale & Montrose Railway" can still be made out under the layers of paint. (Photograph by C. E. Wright; courtesy Mike Morgan.)

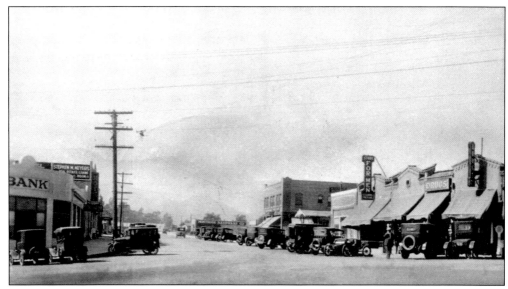

When the founders of Montrose laid out the plans for the "mountain rose," the main business area was supposed to be in the center of the rose around Ocean View and Montrose Avenue. Instead the first businesses in the area opened at Honolulu Avenue and Verdugo Road. When other entrepreneurs built nearby, the business district of Montrose became centered on Honolulu Avenue instead of Montrose Avenue. (Courtesy Glendale Library.)

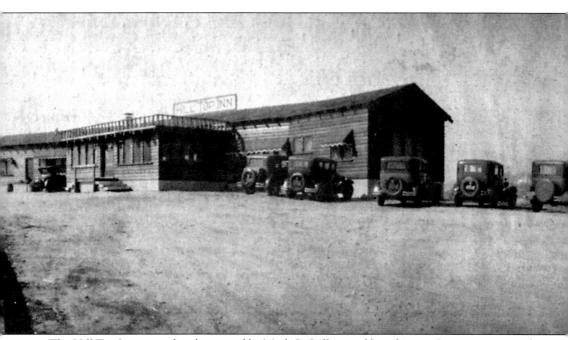

The Hill Top Inn, owned and operated by Mark S. Collins and later his son Stuart, was a popular spot for diners starting in the mid-1920s. The knoll on which it sat was known as Collins Hill. This photograph, taken at the southern edge of the parking lot, looks north toward the mountains. The road at the right is Ocean View Boulevard and the brush-covered area at the right was later developed by the Collins' enterprises. (The area is now covered with apartment buildings.) The

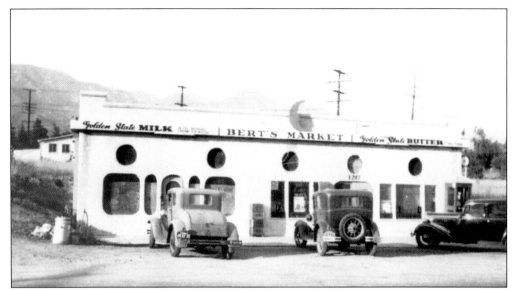

After one too many barroom brawls, the sheriff shut down the Mystic Moon Bar, which served farm workers from the local vineyards. In 1945, Bert LoGuercio opened a store in that building at Pennsylvania and Honolulu Avenue, on the main road to Tujunga. Pete's son took it over in 1968 and ran it for another 20 years. The "moon" still hung over the Bert's Market sign when it first opened.

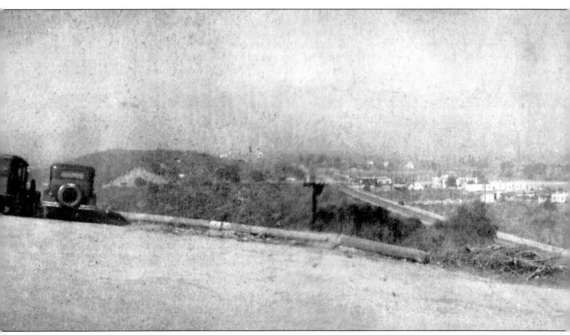

intersection at the right is Foothill and Ocean View Boulevards. The triangular cut in the hillside (Reynolds Hill), made for the widening of Foothill Boulevard, is still visible today. In earlier days, Collins Hill was the site of Easter Sunrise Services sponsored by the Montrose– La Crescenta Kiwanis Club, who erected a tall white cross on the hilltop. Reynolds Hill was used by early Californians to corral sheep.

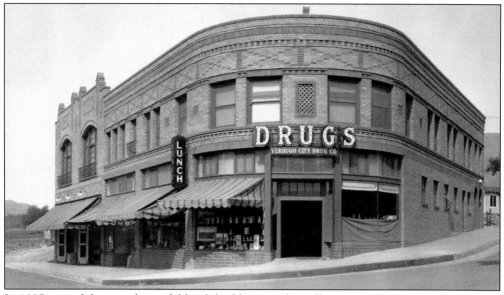

In 1925, one of the most beautiful brick buildings in the valley was built by Harry Fowler, who created it as the centerpiece of his 10-acre development, Verdugo Park (later changed to Verdugo City). Located on the northwest corner of La Crescenta Avenue and Honolulu Avenue, it featured a drugstore with a soda fountain, several storefronts, and an auditorium upstairs. In 1927, guests could sit in the auditorium and listen to live broadcasts of Crescenta Valley's own KGFH radio station. (Courtesy Glendale Library.)

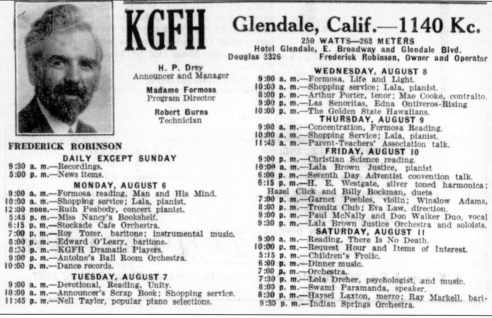

For about two years, La Crescenta had its own radio station—KGFH. Frederick Robinson, an inventor, electronics whiz, and scenic artist for the Lasky Film Company, built a radio tower, studio, and 250-watt transmitter in the backyard of his New York Avenue home. Hundreds of locals showed up to watch the first transmission in 1927. After a couple of years, the station moved to Glendale, but problems with its license caused it to shut down.

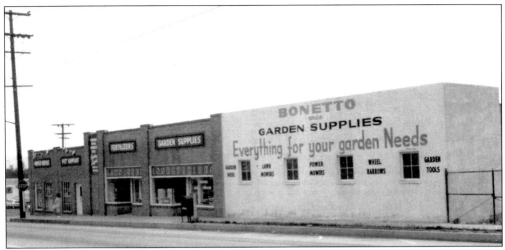

Bonetto's Feed and Fuel store was a landmark in Crescenta Valley for almost 50 years. Started in 1922 by Emil Busch, the business was sold to Tom and Bart Bonetto the next year. In addition to acquiring the business, Tom Bonetto also "acquired" Busch's daughter Florence in marriage. The Bonettos opened the store on the southwest corner of La Crescenta and Montrose Avenues and ran it under slightly different names until 1971, when they retired. (Courtesy Glendale Library.)

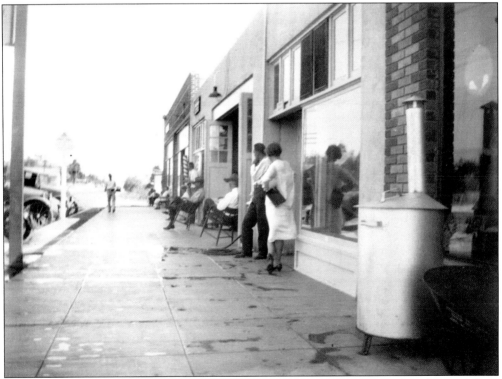

In 1928, this was the business district of La Crescenta. Between Glenwood and Ramsdell on the south side of Foothill Boulevard were the post office, the hardware store, and several other stores. Business must have been a pretty relaxed occupation, based on all the people sitting out in front of their stores. On the right, in front of the hardware store owned by Mr. Laughrey, is a meat smoker. (Courtesy Glendale Library.)

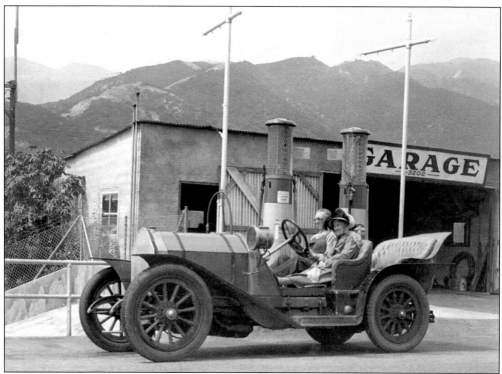

Longtime valley mechanic George Wadey was a collector of vintage automobiles. He is pictured here in the late 1930s, piloting an already antique Fiat race car, once owned by the famous racing pioneer Barney Oldfield, past his garage. (Courtesy Katherine Halford.)

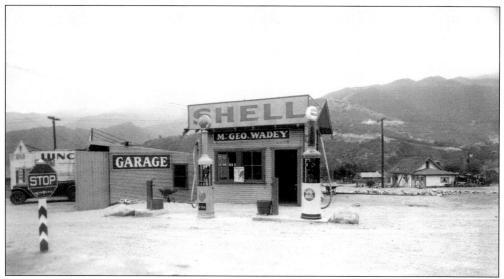

Wadey's service station was located on the southwest corner of Pennsylvania and Honolulu Avenue, which was right on the main route between Glendale and Sunland/Tujunga. Directly behind the gas station on Mills was the Wadey home, plus they owned the Blue Bird Diner that was down around the corner on Pennsylvania. The 1934 flood cut a new channel right between the gas station and diner, destroying their house. (Courtesy Katherine Halford.)

Six
THE WONDER AND FURY OF NATURE

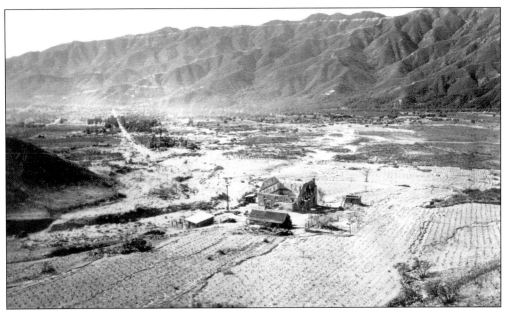

The Crescenta Valley butts up against the mostly undeveloped San Gabriel and Verdugo mountains. As such, residents get to enjoy the incredible beauty of the surroundings, until wind, earthquakes, fires, and floods shatter the tranquility. Shown here is the devastated Le Mesnager barn and vineyards in 1934—a double victim. A fire in November 1933 burned the structure and grapevines and a flood in January 1934 stripped off the topsoil. In this photograph, one can clearly see the lighter colored path of the flood that came out of Dunsmore Canyon and swept straight across the valley toward the Verdugos. It was this flood channel that damaged the back portion of the newly opened Mount Lukens Sanitarium, which sat about where Dunsmore Park is today.

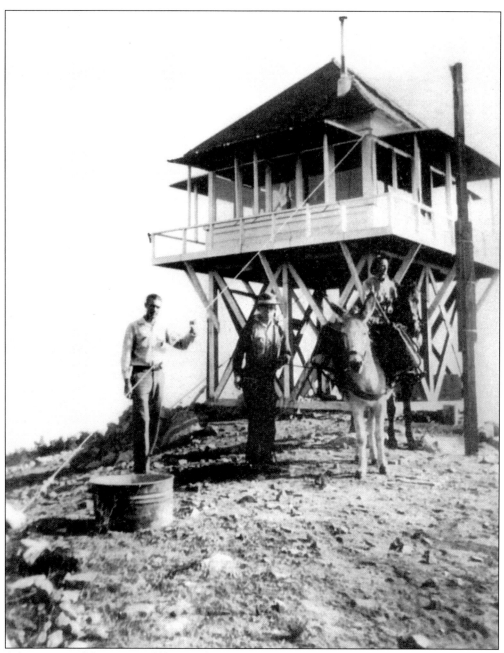

After a series of disastrous wildfires in the mountains and the Crescenta Valley in the late 1800s and early 1900s, an early warning system of fire watchtowers was conceived. In 1923, the peak of Mount Lukens, directly above the Crescenta Valley, received the first of the towers. Pack mules brought supplies to the rangers in the tower. The Crescenta Valley base camp was in the old Briggs barn at the intersection of Freeman and Canyonside on Briggs Terrace. From there the pack mules went up Canyonside, past the Pickens water tunnel, and wound up a steep mountain trail that had been used by locals for decades, and probably by Tongva Indians for hundreds of years before that. While Mount Lukens is still a popular destination for hikers, development has fenced off all access to the historic path. (Courtesy John Robinson.)

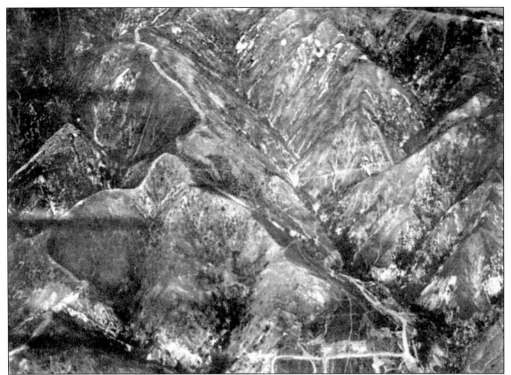

In November 1933, wildfires burned many areas of the San Gabriel Mountains. In Pickens Canyon, it is obvious that the sides of the canyon have been denuded of all heavy vegetation, which led directly to the huge volume of mud, stones, and boulders that were swept down the canyon during the heavy rains a few weeks later on New Year's Eve. (Courtesy Glendale Library.)

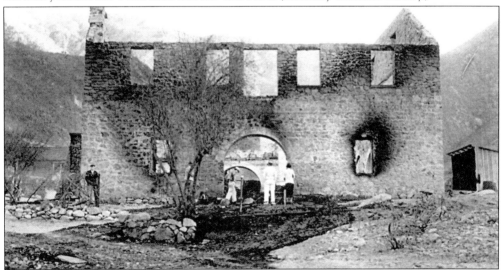

The Le Mesnager barn was used as a winery after Prohibition. Huge fires in November 1933 burned the barn and all the winery equipment inside, ending wine-making operations at this location. The dark stream issuing from the arched doorway is wine—20,000 gallons of it that burst from the burning wooden casks. The Le Mesnagers rebuilt and lived there for another 30 years. (Courtesy Los Angeles Public Library.)

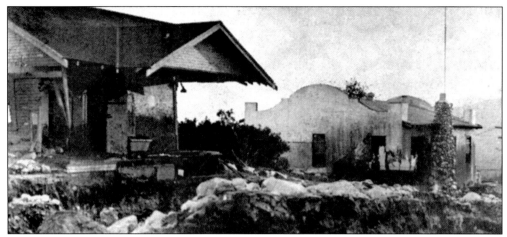

It had been raining heavily on New Year's Eve 1933 and many local citizens were concerned about possible flooding, especially knowing that the mountains had been cleared of nearly all vegetation a few weeks before. As a result, the American Legion Hall on Rosemont Avenue opened for shelter from the rain. But no one anticipated the volume of precipitation and resulting deluge, and the Legion Hall (pictured at right) became a deathtrap.

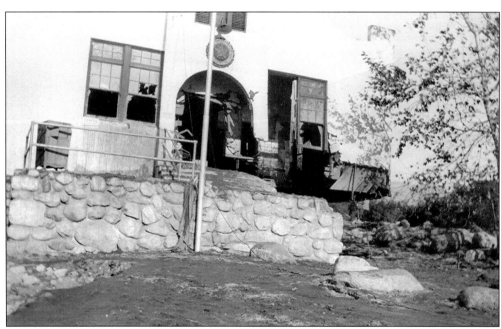

Just after midnight, a record-setting cloudburst in the mountains sent a 10- to 20-foot high wall of water, rocks, and mud hurtling down Pickens Canyon. Houses along the unchanneled streambed were flattened. The flood slammed into the back wall of Legion Hall and ripped into the building. The water, debris, and tangled bodies burst out the front, pictured here.

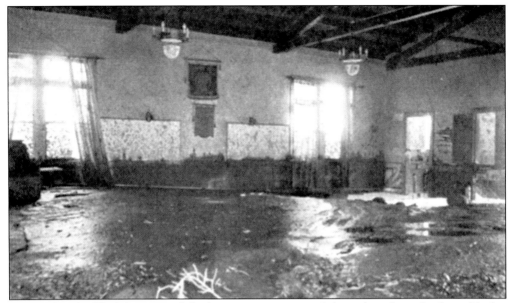

Mud and rocks filled the room while the raging water roared through and out the front. Twelve people inside were killed, including two who were there to help the others. Some survivors managed to escape on their own, while others were swept out the front window. One boy clung to the tree out front and stayed there all night. The tree, visible in the previous photograph, is still there.

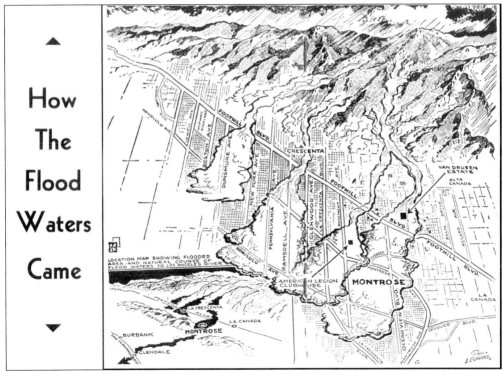

How The Flood Waters Came

This map shows the paths of the floodwaters as they raced down the canyons and into the Crescenta Valley. Pickens Canyon is on the right, with streams pouring into Montrose, including the American Legion Hall.

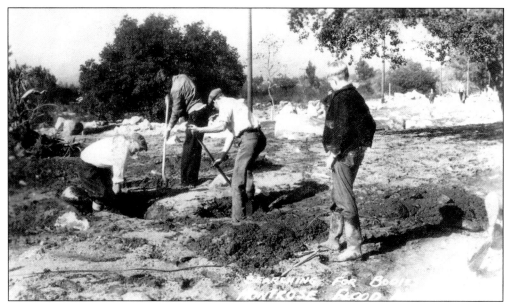

Volunteers dig through the mud in search of victims. An eyewitness reported that as he and neighbors searched for victims the night after the flood surged through town, they managed to rescue one woman buried deep in the mud with only her arm exposed and another woman who had been swept out of the American Legion Hall. These women had seen family, relatives, and friends carried away into the dark. (Courtesy Jerry Weinberg.)

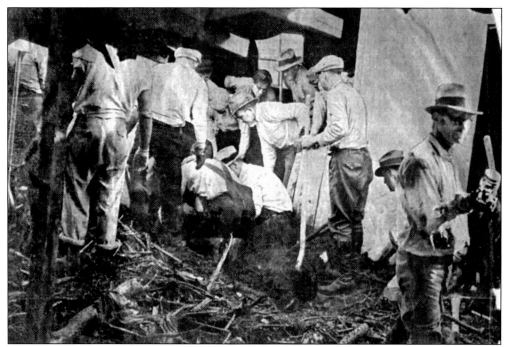

One of the victims of the flood was Eleanor Clark, a choral singer and daughter of Rev. Andy Clark. Reverend Clark and other volunteers found her body in the wreckage of the Montrose Methodist church.

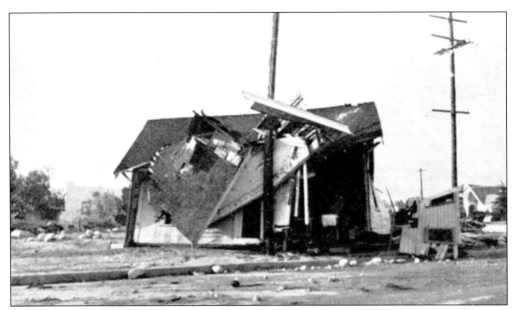

This house was ripped from its footings and carried two blocks with the occupants still inside. It came to a stop as it wrapped around this telephone pole on Montrose Avenue just below Holy Redeemer Church. The total rain that fell in the two hours after midnight was estimated at 13 inches. There were 38 known fatalities, with estimates of many more unknown deaths of squatters who lived in the canyons above La Crescenta. Roughly 400 homes were demolished and an estimated $5 million worth of damage was done.

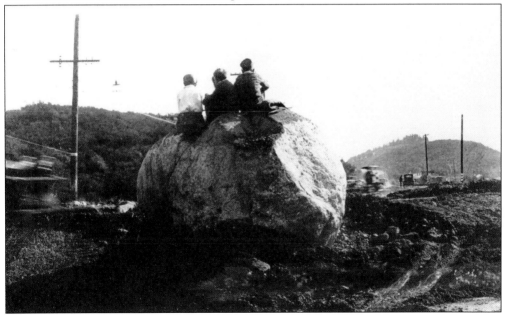

The flood rolled huge boulders down the canyons and onto the streets of Crescenta Valley. After the flood dropped this boulder on Foothill Boulevard at Briggs Avenue, three local boys climbed on top to survey the damage. The middle boy, Gene Rakasits, remembers that local men greased the roadway and pushed the boulder into the gully, which was later filled in. The gas station at Foothill Boulevard and Briggs Avenue was built over it.

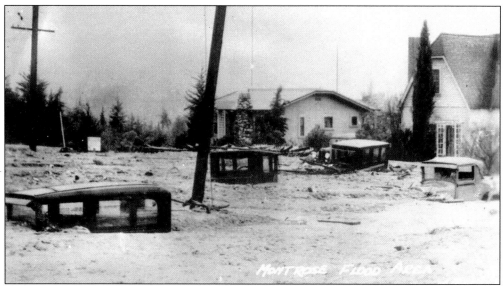
In addition to giant boulders, the flood left behind a thick layer of mud—evidenced here by how high the mud came up on these cars.

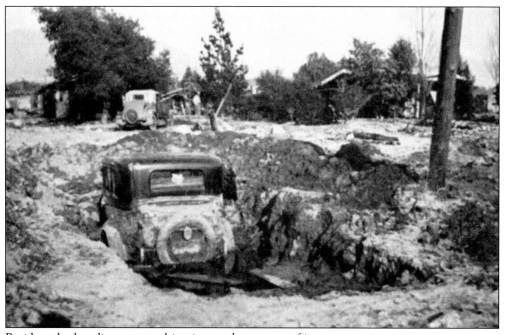
Residents had to dig out everything just to throw most of it away.

C. N. Castor, carrier No. 2 of Montrose, surveyed the damage to determine what houses remained on his route after the flood destroyed so much of the area.

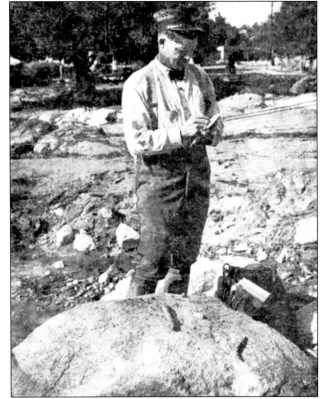

Several groups created different "Flood Souvenir" postcard booklets with photographs and information about the flood. Some were used to raise money for victims, but others were sold by entrepreneurs trying to cash in on the tragedy. This booklet was addressed, but never mailed.

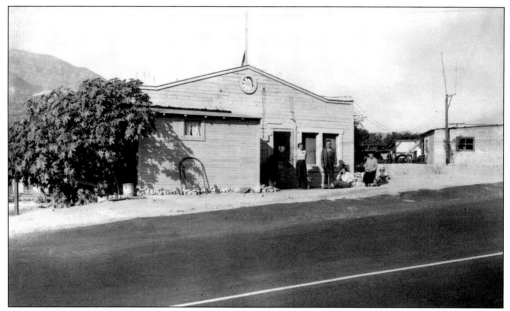

When the 1934 flood destroyed their home, the Wadey family felt lucky to be alive, although they had nowhere to live. They owned the Bluebird Diner, which had escaped the flood relatively intact, so they closed the restaurant, moved in, and lived there for several decades. The old restaurant and home still stands at the intersection of Pennsylvania and Honolulu Avenue as office/retail space. (Courtesy Katherine Halford.)

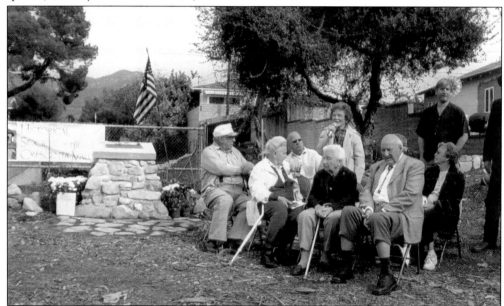

On January 1, 2004, the 70th anniversary of the flood, the Historical Society of the Crescenta Valley dedicated the Flood Memorial to honor the victims and heroes of the flood. Many survivors and family members shared their memories. Pictured here, from left to right, are (first row) Bob Lorenz, Jane Mosher-Usher, Amy Kelly, and Charles Bausback; (second row) Mark Higley, Eloise Benson-Nicholl, Malcolm Benson (obscured), and Maureen Perry. Mark Higley's father was orphaned by the flood and never spoke of it until the anniversary.

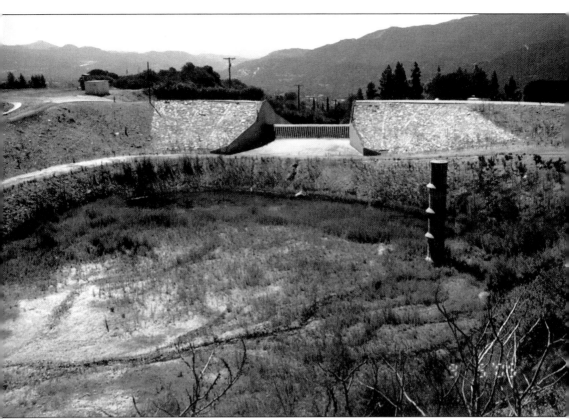

After the great flood, the Army Corps of Engineers analyzed the situation to determine if there was a way to prevent this kind of damage in the future. Nearby Haines Canyon had about the same water surge as Pickens Canyon, but a gravel mining pit near the bottom of Haines Canyon collected most of the mud and rocks, which kept Tujunga from having the same kind of destruction as Montrose. This became the accidental prototype for "debris basins" that the engineers proposed building in the San Gabriel Mountains. They wanted to dig huge bowls at the base of the canyons that would collect mud and rocks while allowing the water to flow through into cement-lined channels. Some residents fiercely opposed the basins because of their ugliness—and the fact that no one was certain they would work. However, the debris basins have worked well. In his book, *The Control of Nature*, author John McPhee wrote extensively about these debris basins.

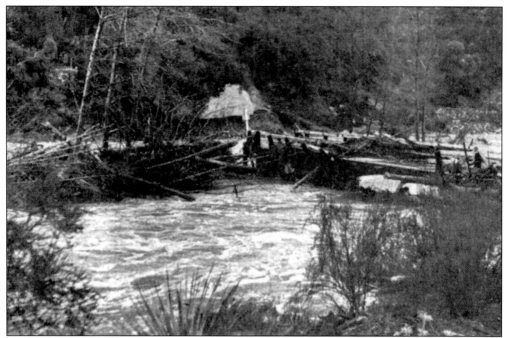

Heavy rains poured down on the Crescenta Valley in January 1969, killing a Montrose Search and Rescue Team member. This photograph shows a washed-out bridge in Big Tujunga Canyon, where several home were destroyed. Homes in Whiting Woods and those close to the mountains in La Crescenta and La Cañada were damaged by sliding and rain-soaked hillsides.

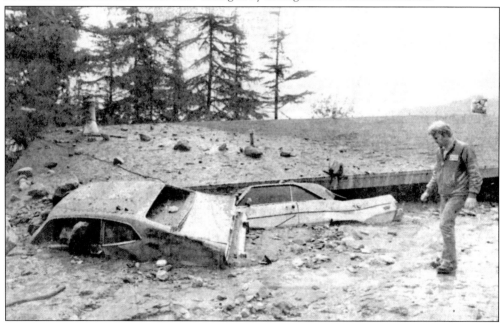

While the debris basins have worked effectively, they can't stop everything. In February 1978, the Shields Canyon dam overflowed and sent water and mud hurtling down Pine Cone Road directly into the Genofile house at the base. No one was seriously injured, but it took the family months to dig out of the mud and repair the damage. (Courtesy La Crescenta Library.)

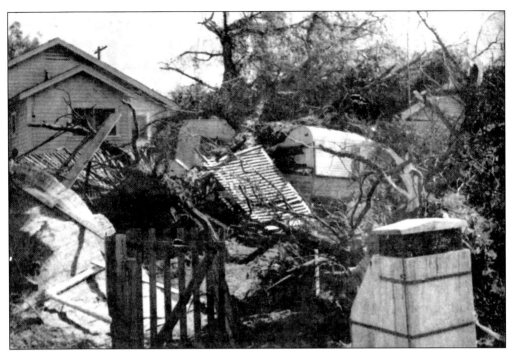

Chicago has nothing on the Crescenta Valley when it comes to high winds. Bounded on the north by the San Gabriel Mountains and the Verdugos to the south, the valley is a natural wind tunnel. Hurricane-like winds hit the area every few years. In March 1964, winds estimated between 80 and 100 miles per hour tore through the area, knocking down trees and ripping off roofs.

In April 1973, another fierce windstorm hit the area, uprooting and tossing this large tree into the empty swimming pool at Mountain Oaks Park at the south end of New York Avenue. The storm caused several electrical outages in addition to uprooting and destroying many trees. However, old-timers insist that windstorms are not as fierce as they used to be because of the number of new trees. (Courtesy Glendale Library.)

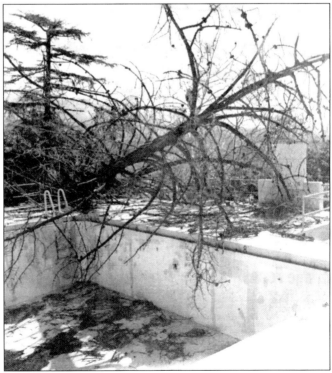

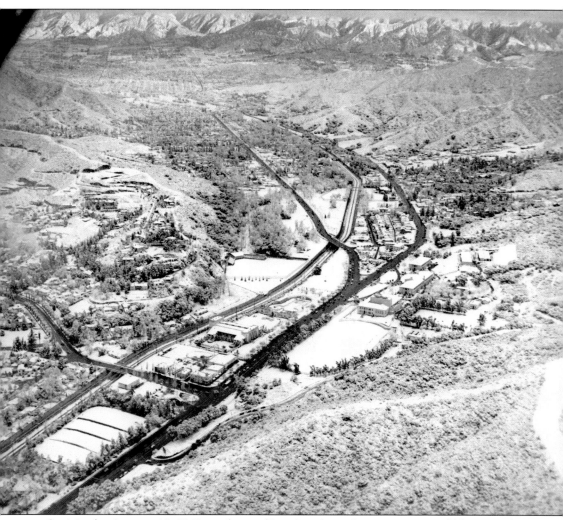

On Monday, January 10, 1949, residents of Los Angeles woke up to an incredibly rare sight—a blanket of snow covering just about everything from the San Gabriel Mountains to Long Beach. This helicopter shot over the Glendale Community College area shows Verdugo Road in the foreground heading into Montrose and the Crescenta Valley. Almost five inches of snow fell in the Glendale flatlands and much more than that fell above Foothill Boulevard. With temperatures hovering around 28 degrees, radiators froze and cars slid all over the roads. There were many accidents, but no fatalities. Growers feared the worst for their fruit trees, but most suffered little damage as the snow insulated the branches from the cold. Over the next two days, snow fell in the San Fernando Valley and the Los Angeles Unified School District did something it had never done before (or since)—declared a snow day. (Courtesy Glendale Library.)

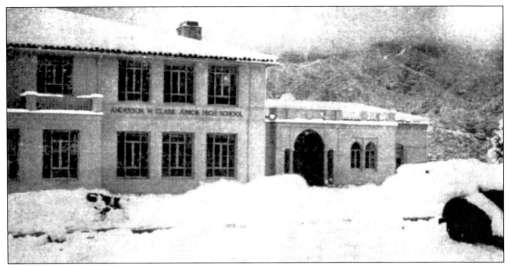

Because no one ever imagined that much snow could accumulate in the valley, schools were not prepared; they expected students to attend classes. While many showed up, they couldn't concentrate so the teachers let them out to enjoy a good snowball fight in the unusual snowscape. There was so much snow that some were able to make snowmen.

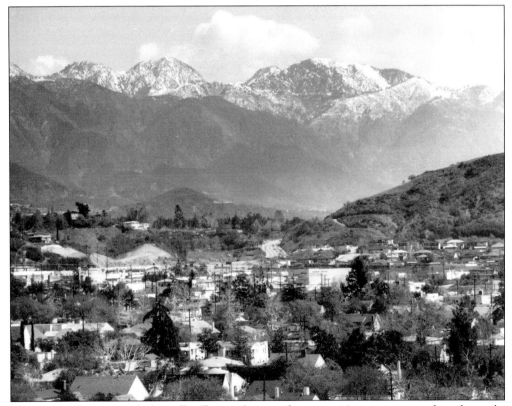

While snow flurries reach the valley floor only every few years, it's a rare winter when the peaks of the San Gabriels are not covered (or at least dusted) in white. Snow sports are available by taking a short drive up the Angeles Crest Highway.

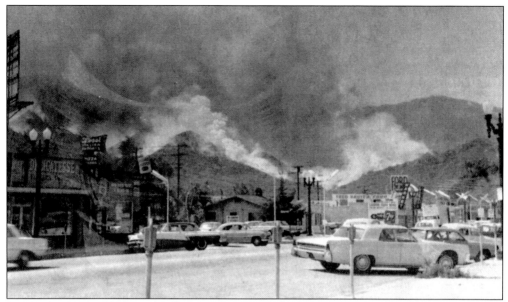

In March 1964, wildfires came dangerously close to downtown Montrose. As hot winds gusted close to 100 miles per hour, sparks and embers were blown everywhere and business owners were ready to evacuate. A shift in the wind forced the fire away from the town, but at least 15 houses were destroyed in the area.

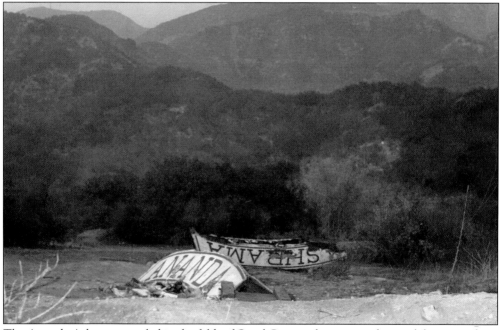

The Ananda Ashrama, nestled in the folds of Quail Canyon, has survived several disastrous fires. The most dramatic took place in November 1933. As flames shot 100 feet into the sky, the religious community members retreated to the cloister, where they fervently chanted prayers. Firefighters outside lay facedown on the ground while the fire swirled over them. The fire stormed across the compound, burning all the vegetation to a fine white ash, but miraculously left the buildings untouched. (Courtesy Glendale Library.)

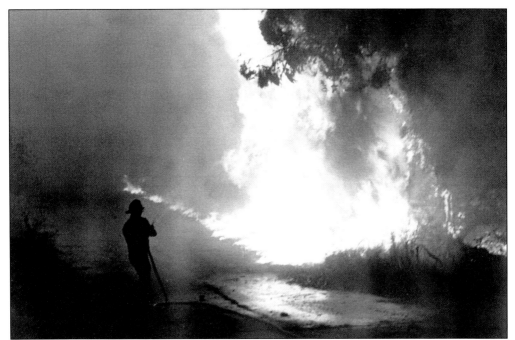

In 1975, a professional firefighter tries to dampen this wildfire. Almost 50 years earlier in 1926, a fire burned through the same area, but volunteers fought the fire then. Traffic was stopped and all men were pressed into service, no matter how they were dressed. Men in suits and tuxedoes threw dirt or heaved wet sacks under the direction of the Angeles Forest Protective Association. (Courtesy Glendale Library.)

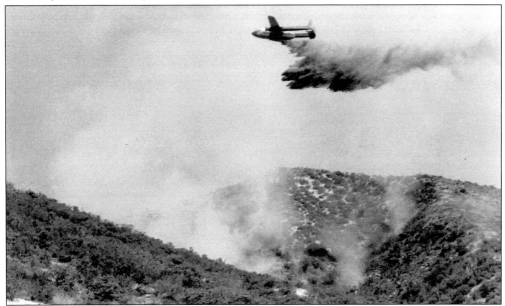

In the summer of 1977, a C119 Fairchild "Flying Boxcar" drops water on a wildfire in the Angeles National Forest above Crescenta Valley. This and other World War II–era airplanes were pressed into service as firefighting tankers in the postwar years. The age of the planes and the rugged service demands resulted in several crashes in the San Gabriel Mountains. (Courtesy Glendale Library.)

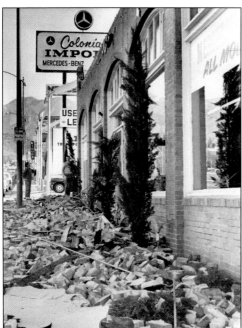

In February 1971, the Sylmar earthquake shook the Crescenta Valley hard, cracking homes, tumbling chimneys, and showering sidewalks with bricks and debris from many business storefronts. This photograph shows the front of Colonial Buick on Verdugo Road in Montrose. (Courtesy Glendale Library.)

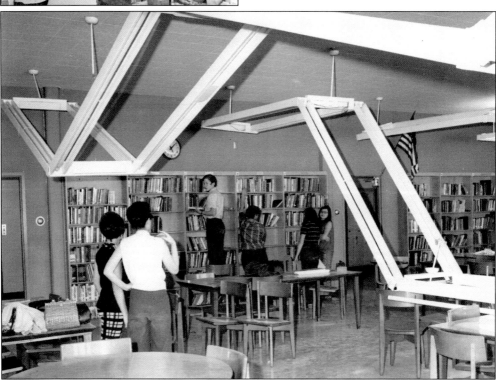

Most southern California school children don't wake up with the hopes of a snow day being declared to keep them out of school. After the Sylmar earthquake damaged Clark Junior High in 1971, the school had to shut down for repairs. While not much good came from the shaker, the kids were able to enjoy their "earthquake days"—even if they had to be made up later on. (Courtesy Glendale Library.)

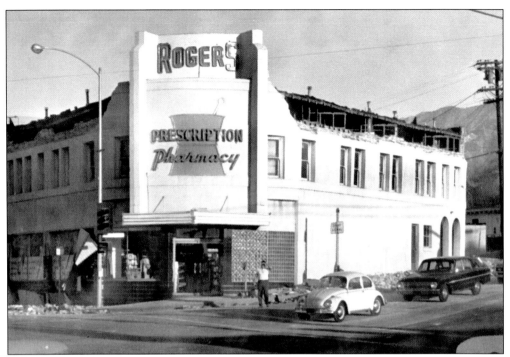

The 1971 Sylmar earthquake had a devastating effect on the brick buildings of the Crescenta Valley. The striking Roger's Pharmacy building at La Crescenta and Honolulu Avenues was undermined so badly that it had to be demolished. On the remaining brick buildings in the valley, earthquake retrofit measures included covering up beautiful facades with stucco to hold the bricks together. (Courtesy Glendale Library.)

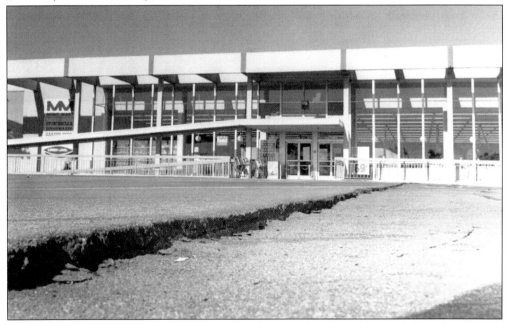

The Sylmar earthquake created yet another level in the parking lot at the Merit Mart (now OSH). (Courtesy Glendale Library.)

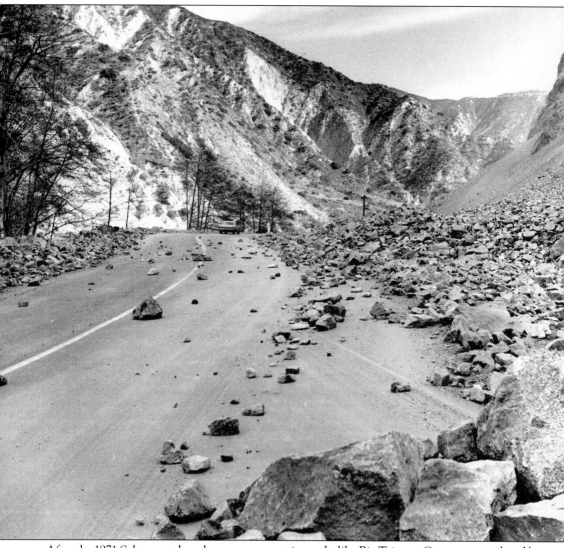

After the 1971 Sylmar earthquake, many mountain roads, like Big Tujunga Canyon, were closed by landslides. The San Gabriel Mountain range is one of the fastest growing in the world and when the mountains are thrust upward by an earthquake, the violent shaking shatters the granite into pieces that eventually tumble (or wash) down into the valley. This rocky soil has prompted many a frustrated gardener to refer to the area as "Rock Crescenta." (Courtesy Glendale Library.)

Seven
The Good, the Sad, and the Seedy

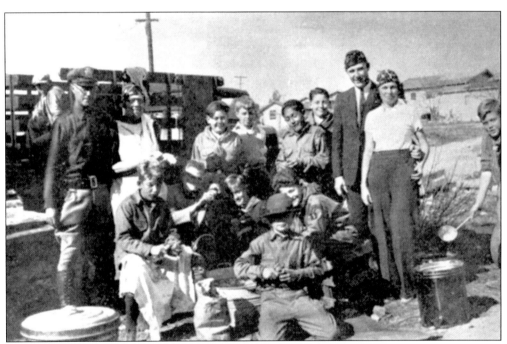

As in all disasters, the great flood of 1934 brought out the good and bad in residents of the valley. Here is a troop of local Boy Scouts who have mobilized to distribute food to victims of the flood. The disaster attracted hundreds of volunteers to help dig out the community, plus thousands of sightseers hoping to find souvenirs of the event, causing the sheriff to close off the area. While some men ventured in the dark and wet minutes after the disaster to help find survivors, others came out to loot. One survivor remembers returning to his damaged home to find a group of women fighting over his mother's clothing. Another one remembers pulling a woman with two broken legs from her car and having to threaten to break down the door of a nearby house to gain admittance for the injured woman. But overall the community rallied to help each other and rebuild.

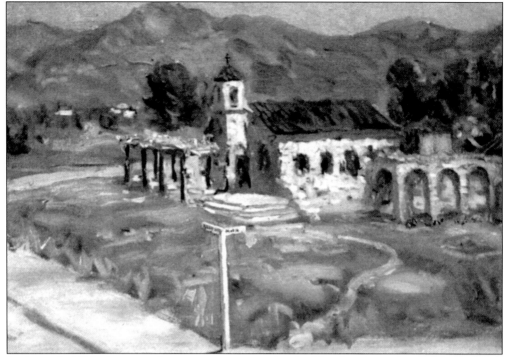

In the early 1920s, knowing the community wanted to build a church on the northeast corner of Rosemont Avenue and Foothill Boulevard, artist Seymour Thomas set up his easel across the street and painted his vision—a stone church patterned after ones he had seen in the French countryside. He brought the still wet painting to the planning meeting and all enthusiastically approved. St. Luke's was built as it was shown in the painting, which now hangs in the church office. (Courtesy La Crescenta Library.)

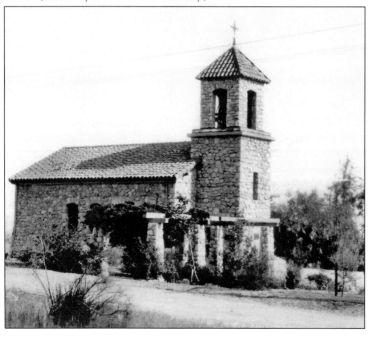

Seymour Thomas carried chalk in his pocket and on his strolls across the valley would mark a blue cross on the stones he wanted for the construction of St. Luke's. When parishioners came across these marked stones, they carried them to the church site. The church, actually a stone facade over a wood frame, was dedicated in 1924. This church is the architectural landmark of the valley. (Courtesy Frank Boyer.)

Swami Paramananda came to the United States from India in 1906 to promote the teachings of the Vedanta Society, an eclectic religion that used meditation and yoga to gain enlightenment by combining all the world's religions. He established a church in Boston and, by the late 1910s, wished to open a branch on the west coast. He loved the Crescenta Valley and spent much time hiking in the mountains. (Courtesy Aranda Ashram.)

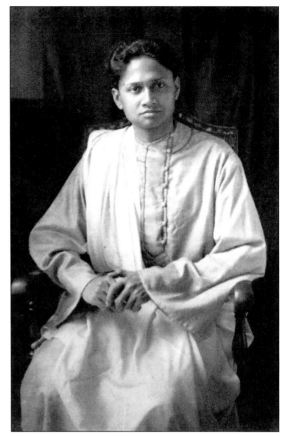

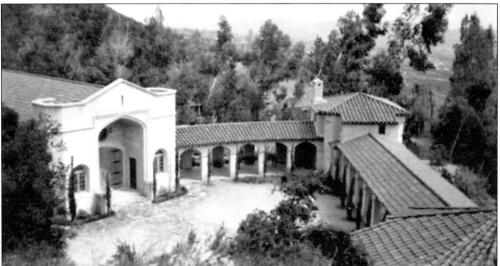

In 1923, Swami Paramananda attended an afternoon tea held by artist Seymour Thomas at his home in La Crescenta. Thomas knew that the Fusenot Ranch, built in 1919, was on the market, and the swami bought it immediately. The ranch, with its own water source and orchards, was quickly enlarged, culminating with the construction of this temple in 1928. The religious order has existed in harmony with the surrounding community ever since. (Courtesy Aranda Ashram.)

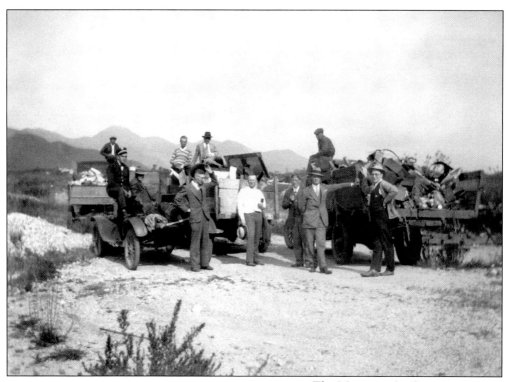

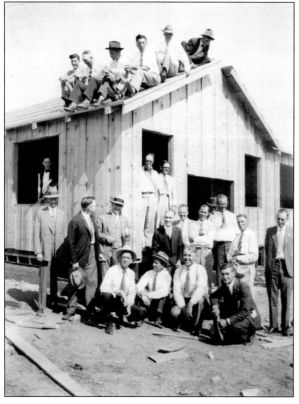

The Montrose–La Crescenta Kiwanis Club, a major service organization in La Crescenta, formed in 1925. Anybody who was anybody in the Crescenta Valley was in the Kiwanis Club. Here in the early 1930s, members of the Kiwanis Cleanup Squad, decked out in suits and ties, pick up trash around the valley. (Courtesy Glendale Library.)

In September 1927, the Montrose–La Crescenta Kiwanis Club built the "Scout Cabin" which was used for many years by various scouting units of the La Crescenta area. It originally stood on Ramsdell Avenue near the intersection of Ramsdell and Community Street. The structure was later moved to the grounds of Andersen W. Clark Junior High School, where it was used for various purposes before being torn down. (Courtesy Glendale Library.)

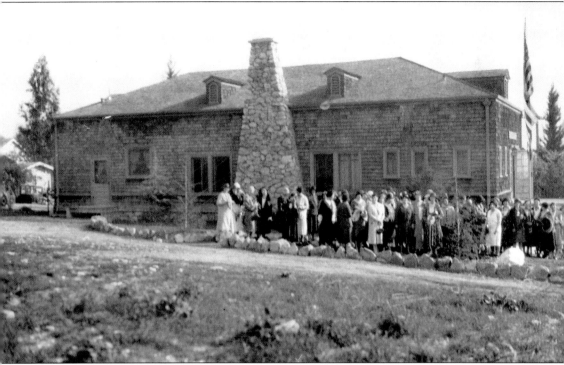

Begun in 1911 as the Crescenta Club to help and improve the community, the La Crescenta Women's Club, pictured here, was incorporated in 1923 with the official objectives of "advancement in all lines of general culture, promotion of the general welfare of the community and philanthropy work." Initial projects included making improvements to the La Crescenta School and offering aid during the Big Tujunga fire of 1925. After the great flood in 1934, the Woman's Club served as a first aid station. The clubhouse was built in 1925 and enlarged in 1961, as the club celebrated its 50th anniversary. Damaged significantly in 1966 by an arson-set fire, it was rebuilt almost immediately. (Courtesy Glendale Library.)

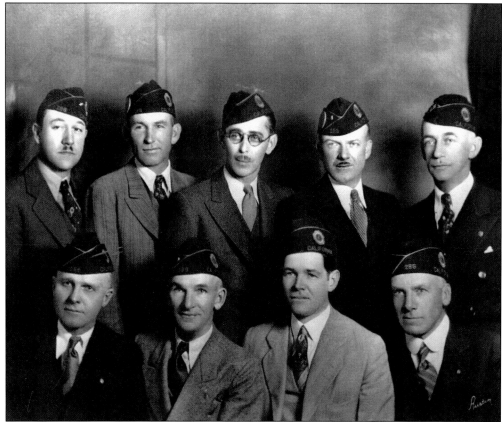

The American Legion Post 288 was founded in 1924 by World War I veterans living in the Crescenta Valley. The initial meeting was held at the Sparr Heights Community Building. One of the post's earliest endeavors was sponsoring Montrose Boy Scout Troop No. 1. (Courtesy Glendale Library.)

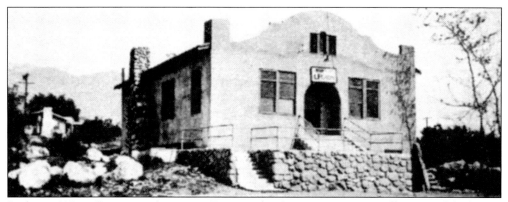

Built in 1925 on Rosemont Avenue at Fairway, the American Legion Hall was used for legion meetings and other community events. In 1934, the hall was destroyed by the great flood. In response to this disaster, Tom Bonetto donated land on La Crescenta Avenue for a new building, constructed out of wood from the old structure. It opened on April 10, 1935, with Comdr. Tom Bonetto presiding. (Courtesy Glendale Library.)

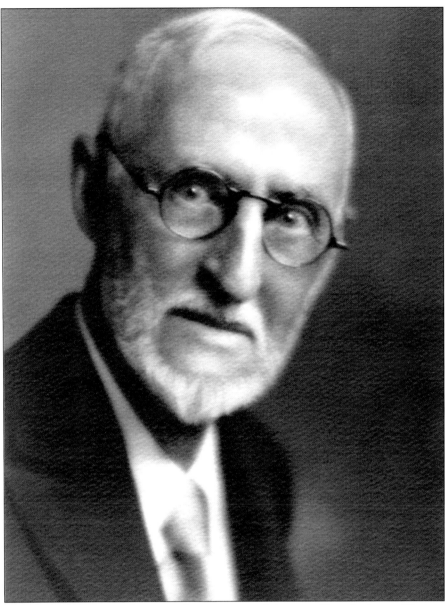

In spite of his two doctorate degrees and many accomplishments, Rev. Andersen Clark insisted that everyone call him Andy. He grew up in Illinois and his father was friends with Abraham Lincoln, who marked Andy's growth on the door frame of the Clark home. After getting his Ph.D. from the University of Nebraska, Andy founded the Child Saving Institute in Omaha, where he helped place approximately 4,000 unwanted children into good homes. When World War I broke out, Andy volunteered and became the oldest man to receive an overseas commission. He retired to the Crescenta Valley in 1922, living in a modest house in Montrose. He delivered food baskets to needy families and spoke at local schools. He was vacationing in Palm Springs the night of the great flood. His daughter died that night, his son was injured, and his home was destroyed. In spite of these setbacks, he continued to serve the community. Andy died in April 1938 at the age of 86. Later that year, La Crescenta Junior High was renamed Andersen W. Clark Junior High School. (Courtesy Glendale School District.)

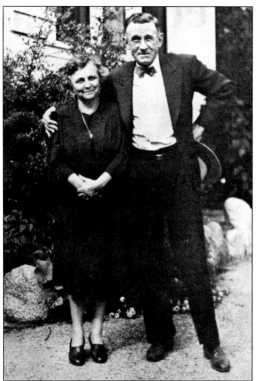

Art and Grace Carpenter moved into the caretaker's cottage of the Gould Castle when they first arrived here from Washington, D.C. In 1922, Grace got a job as a reporter with the brand new *La Crescenta Valley Ledger*. In 1928, the Carpenters bought *The Ledger* and ran it successfully for decades, turning the business over to their son Don, who was the editor until the 1980s when it went out of business. Grace Carpenter had a love for local history, and, indeed, much of the recorded history of the Crescenta Valley today (including this book) is due to her interviews with valley pioneers and her many articles covering the heritage of La Crescenta.

In front of Clark Junior High, two teams' cans from a food drive are laid out in long lines to determine the winning side. Representatives of the winners hold their hands high in celebration while the "loser" feigns disappointment. In reality, of course, everyone won. (Courtesy Glendale School District.)

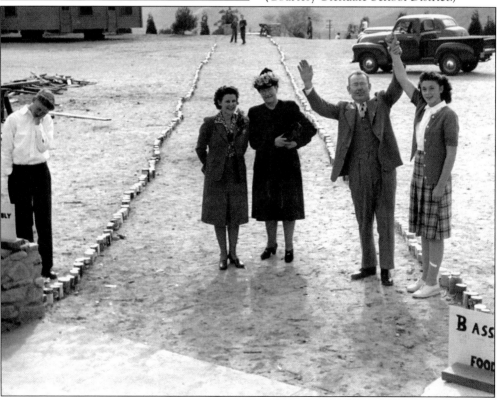

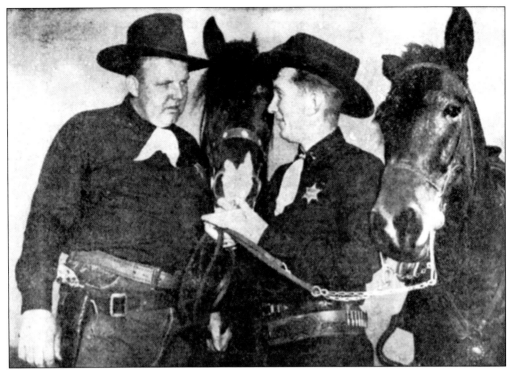

As incongruous as the name may seem today, the Montrose Mounted Posse played an important role in the search and rescue of people lost or stranded in the mountains surrounding the valley. In this photograph from the rodeo program, Capt. A. J. McLaren outlines a search for Lt. Bob Huntington. (Courtesy Jean Maluccio.)

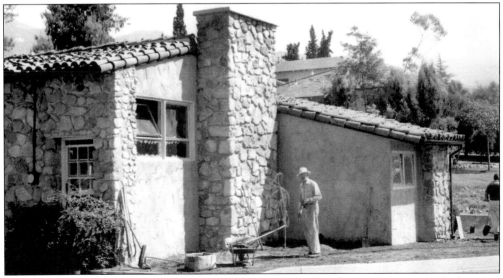

Originally built to house Fire Station No. 19 in 1930, this building was constructed of natural stone to match its nearest neighbor, St. Luke's Episcopal Church. When Foothill Boulevard was widened in the late 1940s, the fire station lost its front driveway. Since they were outgrowing the small station, Los Angeles County sold it to St. Luke's Church, which has used it as a youth house, Boy Scout meeting place, and Sunday school. (Courtesy St. Luke's Episcopal Church.)

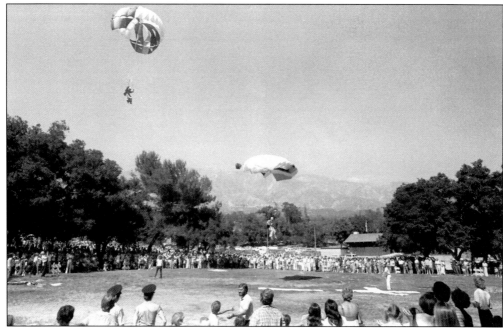

In 1973, Tim Richards, a popular Crescenta Valley High School football player, suffered a paralyzing spinal injury during a game. The community rallied around the wheelchair-bound boy and created the Tim Richards Foundation to benefit area youth who had suffered crippling injuries. In 1975, 30,000 people attended the Tim Richards Friendship Fair, a two-day event held in Crescenta Valley Park. (Courtesy Glendale Library.)

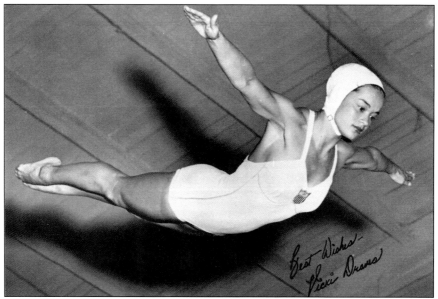

Vicki Manalo, a young high diver, encountered discrimination at swimming stadiums because of her Filipino descent. In the early 1940s, she met and married Lyle Draves, the swim instructor at Crescenta Valley's Indian Springs swimming pool, which she used for training. At the 1948 Olympics in London, she won double gold in diving, becoming the first Asian American to win an Olympic gold medal.

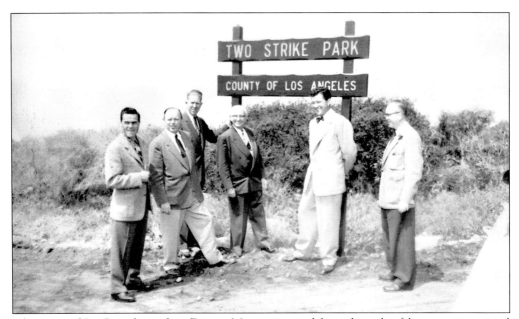

Film star and La Cañada resident Dennis Morgan, second from the right, felt more recreational areas were needed for the area's growing youth population, saying that any kid who had to play out in the streets "already had two strikes against him." Morgan, the unofficial mayor of Crescenta Valley, organized exhibition baseball games featuring celebrity friends and professional athletes to raise money for Two Strike Park, which opened on Rosemont Avenue in the late 1950s. (Courtesy Glendale Library.)

In 1980, the Houk family—descendents of the Felhaubers, Crescenta Valley pioneers—donated a portion of their property on Tujunga Canyon Road below Foothill Boulevard to become Felhauber Houk Park. A plaque was placed in the park describing the history of the Felhauber family. This park demonstrates the complexity of civic boundaries in La Crescenta. Although geographically the park is in the Crescenta Valley, it is administered by the City of Los Angeles and its post office address is Tujunga. (Courtesy Glendale Library.)

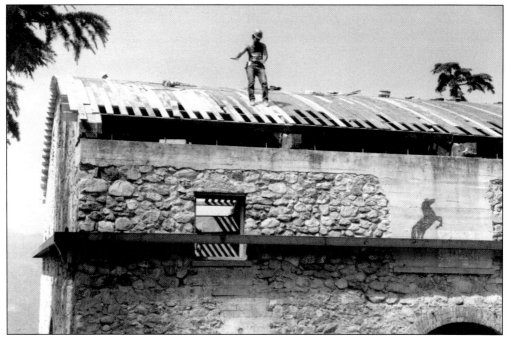

The Le Mesnager barn survived Prohibition, fires, floods, and earthquakes, but nearly did not survive a developer's wrecking ball in the 1980s. Fortunately the City of Glendale purchased the 700-acre site for use as a park and bolted steel beams to sides of the barn to stabilize the structure seismically. The beams will be removed as the building undergoes a more complex seismic retrofit by the city in coming years. (Courtesy Glendale Library.)

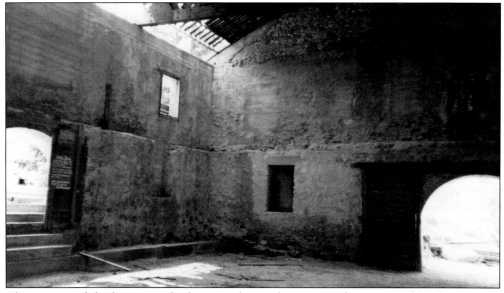

The interior of the barn once had a second story living area that was used by the son and grandson of George Le Mesnager from the 1930s until its sale in the late 1960s. After that, the barn was used to stable horses. The City of Glendale acquired the barn as the centerpiece of the Deukmajian Wilderness Park and plans to refurbish the historic structure for use as a community center. (Courtesy Glendale Library.)

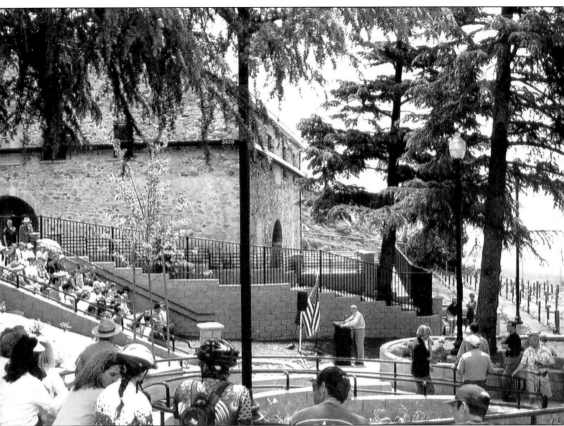

On May 15, 2004, former governor George Deukmajian addressed the crowd at the rededication of the Deukmajian Wilderness Park. The 702-acre recreational area is on grounds that once belonged to the George Le Mesnager family. Le Mesnager grew grapes on this property as well as down the hill in Glendale (and a few other locations) for his winery. The last of the Le Mesnager family moved out in 1968 and leased the land to an equestrian center. Twenty years later, a developer tried to subdivide the grounds and build hundreds of homes, but the City of Glendale, with a grant from the Santa Monica Mountains Conservancy, bought it instead. The park was first opened in 1989 with just hiking and equestrian trails. The city recently added paved roads and parking lots, lights, picnic tables, and an outdoor amphitheater—hence the rededication. One proposed plan is to convert the old barn into a small wine-making museum to reflect the history of both the property and one of the early industries of the area.

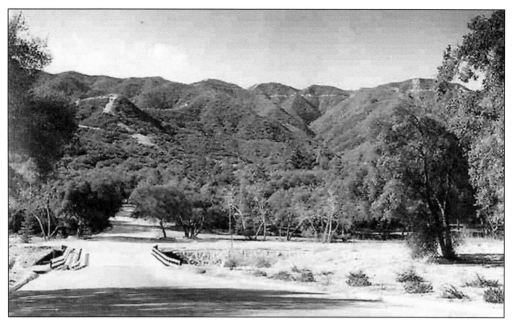

Whiting Woods (shown here in the 1930s) had a scandalous beginning. In 1915, Perry Whiting acquired the property in a court sale. Called the Pasadena Gun Club, it was really a brothel and speakeasy where a man had been shot during a fight. Whiting built a beautiful home and lived here quietly until the property was developed in the 1950s and 1960s.

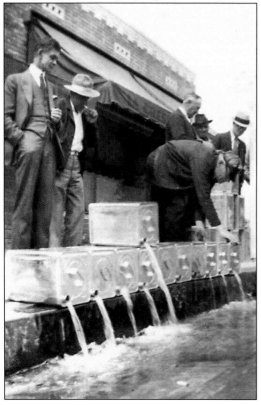

Local law officers supervise the dumping of confiscated homemade whiskey in front of the Montrose Sheriff Station on the west side of Ocean View just above Honolulu Avenue. During Prohibition, the Crescenta Valley was isolated enough for moonshiners to produce their wares yet close enough to Los Angeles to distribute it. Stills and speakeasies thrived here in the 1920s, but occasionally someone got caught. (Courtesy Glendale Library.)

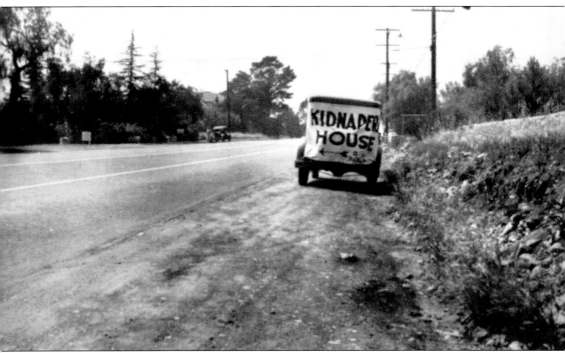

In May 1934, Beverly Hills millionaire William F. Gettle was kidnapped from his Arcadia estate by three men and taken to a rented house on Rosemont Avenue in La Crescenta. They demanded $60,000 in ransom money and held Mr. Gettle captive for five days before police discovered the location. They surrounded the house and captured the three men without the ransom being paid. Curiosity seekers flocked from all over to see the house—so many that the owner opened up the home for people to see the bedroom in which the victim was held. He also draped this sign over a car to signal the location. (Courtesy Glendale Library.)

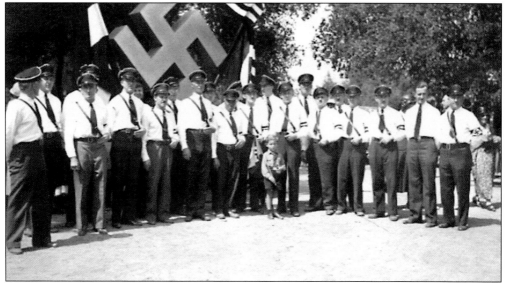

Hindenberg Park, owned by the German American League, hosted several infamous rallies in the late 1930s by the Bund, an American political group styling itself after the Nazis. The park was named for German president Paul Von Hindenberg, who died in 1934, and featured a huge five-foot tall bust of him that was regularly vandalized during World War II. The bust was removed when the county bought the park in the 1950s. It was renamed Crescenta Valley Park. (Courtesy CSUN.)

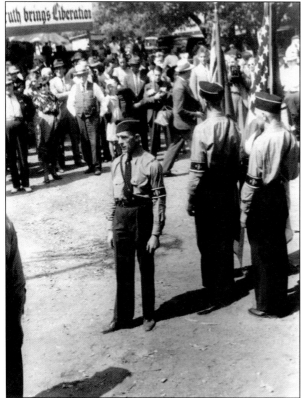

The Bund rallies drew thousands of spectators and lent a seamy reputation to a park that had been no more than a lovely site for German cultural celebrations, with oompah bands and kegs of German beer. Several old-timers remember the Bund practice of "snow-storming," where a hired airplane would fly over the Crescenta Valley during these rallies, dropping thousands of pro-Nazi leaflets. (Courtesy CSUN.)

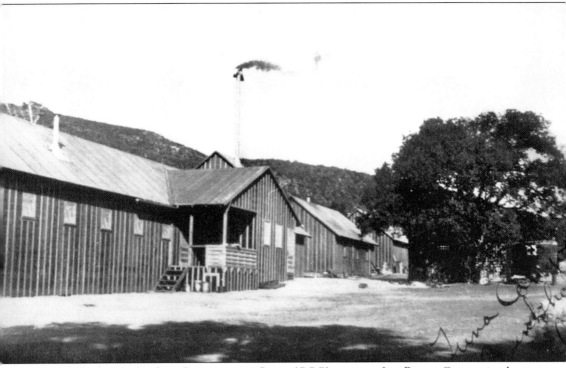

Originally built as a Civilian Conservation Corps (CCC) camp in Las Barras Canyon in the 1930s, "Tuna Camp" was taken over by the Department of Justice and the INS on December 8, 1941, in an immediate response to the bombing of Pearl Harbor. A 12-foot barbed wire fence was erected and the camp received prisoners on December 16. The seven-barrack camp was run by the Immigration Service and housed mostly Japanese. However, the 300-man capacity camp was also temporary home to other "enemy aliens" such as Italians, Poles, Germans, and South Americans. A few American Nazis that had posed for photographs in Hindenberg Park a couple of years before ended up here as well. Prisoners were moved from here to other detention camps such as Manzanar after they had been built. The Verdugo Hills Golf Course now occupies the old "Tuna Camp" site at the intersection of Tujunga Canyon Road and La Tuna Canyon Road. (Courtesy Little Landers.)

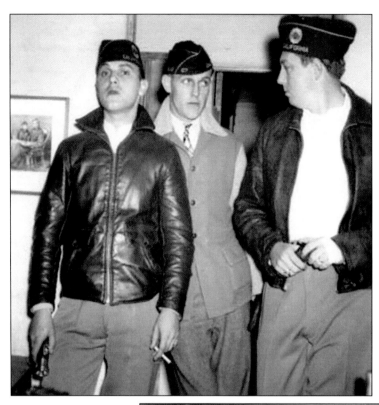

In November 1947, members of the American Legion broke into the home of Hugh Hardyman during a meeting of the Crescenta Valley Democratic Club. Convinced that the club supported the overthrow of the U.S. government, 20 local American Legion members stationed themselves by the doors and windows. Their leader pushed Hardyman aside and told the club members to go home "and thank God that you live in the United States!" (Courtesy Katherine Halford.)

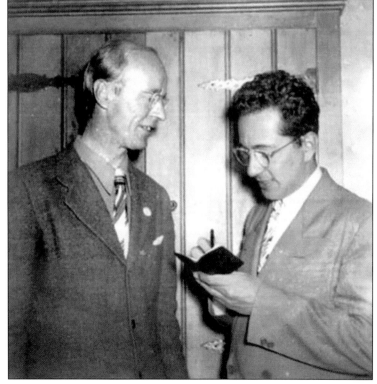

Hardyman, left, was a liberal activist who had gained fame at San Pedro's infamous Liberty Hill strike. At a union rally, Upton Sinclair read from the Bill of Rights and was arrested for "suspicion of criminal syndicalism." Two more speakers protested and were arrested. Hugh Hardyman took the podium, commented on the fine weather that day, and was also arrested. Those arrests sparked the formation of the ACLU. (Courtesy Katherine Halford.)

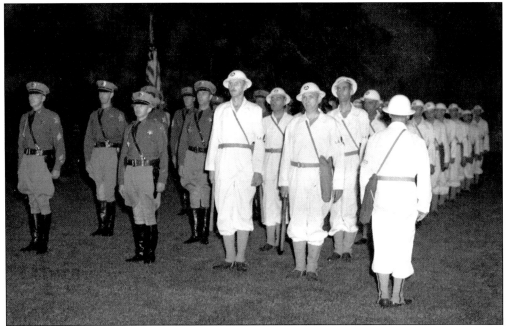

In the 1950s, as the cold war with the Soviet Union heated up, La Crescenta remained alert. Civil defense drills, like the nighttime one shown above, were held on local school grounds.

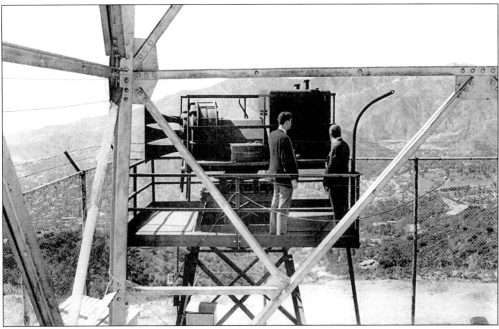

Because the threat of a nuclear attack from the Soviet Union was very real for residents in the 1950s and 1960s, 180-horsepower attack-warning sirens were installed in the hills around the valley. The County Office of Civil Defense orchestrated regular drills of the civic defense system, including the sounding off of this powerful siren, during which elementary school children were instructed to move away from the windows at their schools and crouch down with their hands covering their heads. (Courtesy Los Angeles Public Library.)

> Said deed further provides for reversion of title upon breach of the following provisions:- "That the parties of second part shall not convey, sell or lease or otherwise dispose of said premises, or any part thereof to any person not of the White or Caucasian race, nor shall any person other than of the White or Caucasian race acquire said property or any portion thereof or any interest therein by purchase, lease or otherwise."

Racial covenants were common in property deeds in the Crescenta Valley (and in many parts of California) into the 1950s. In 1941, because an African American family attempted to buy a home in La Cañada, a mass meeting of local residents was called, urging the enforcement of racial restrictions contained in their deeds. In 1953, the U.S. Supreme Court made the enforcement of such covenants illegal, although they still appear in older deeds.

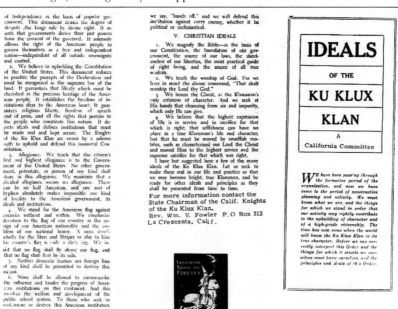

The Ku Klux Klan has been a shadowy presence in the valley since the 1910s, surfacing on several occasions. In 1924, a two-day rally was held in the San Rafael Mountains, complete with burning crosses. In 1966, this pamphlet originating from La Crescenta was distributed by the California Knights of the Ku Klux Klan. The Klan erupted again in 1983 when a small rally in Sunland attracted nationwide attention. (Courtesy CSUN.)

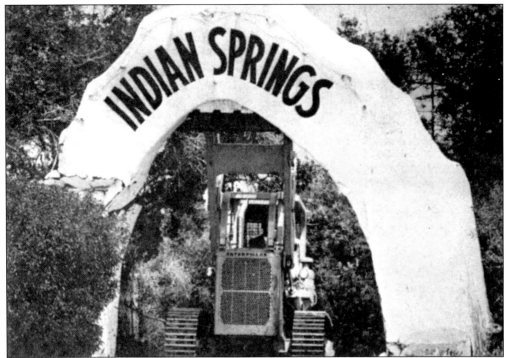

In 1966, the Indian Springs resort and recreation center on Verdugo Road was dug up, filled in, and replaced by a shopping center. It's called the Indian Springs Shopping Center, but ivy covers the sign so most residents only know it by the stores' names (like Vons, Sav-On, Billy's, Radio Shack, and Subway) and are unaware that the flat parking lot was once a deep wooded canyon with a natural spring.

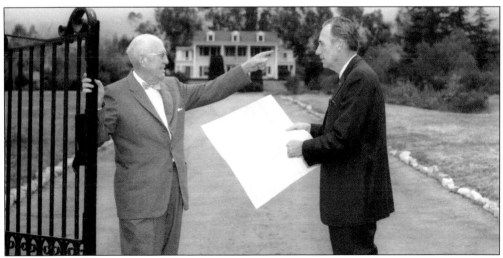

As the baby boom boomed, new schools were needed. The Glendale School District eyed the Bishop Mansion and its five acres on Mountain Avenue. The Bishops were unwilling sellers so in 1964, the GUSD forced the sale under eminent domain. Here we see William Bishop on the left, and Mike Hesse, GUSD business manager, discussing the situation. The house was demolished and Mountain Avenue Elementary School opened on the site in 1967. (Courtesy Glendale Library.)

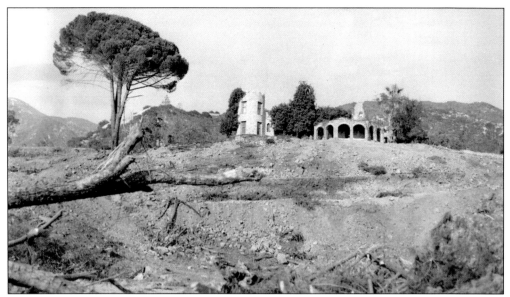

This is the last look at the grand Gould Castle in 1955 before the subdivision above Castle Road was started. Although the remains of the castle were bulldozed into an adjacent canyon, the tree next to the castle was left untouched. Even today, if one turns right on Canalda, off Ocean View, and looks up the hill, the distinctive umbrella shaped crown of the Italian Stone Pine can still be seen. (Courtesy Glendale Library.)

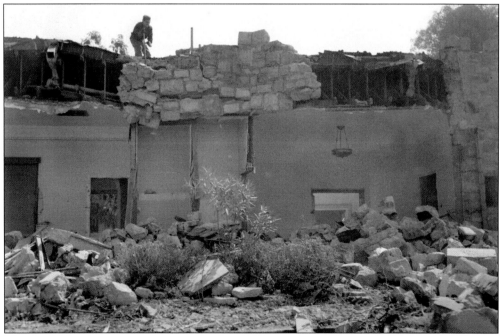

The Gould Castle was torn down in October 1955 to make way for a new subdivision at the top of Ocean View. The Crescenta Valley did little to preserve its heritage in the building boom years of the 1950s and 1960s. The 1881 Briggs Home, the 1886 Holly House, the 1890 La Crescenta Hotel, the 1886 Villa Esperanza, the first 1886 schoolhouse, and 1929 Indian Springs all fell without protest. (Courtesy Glendale Library.)

Eight
THE SHIFT FROM RURAL TO SUBURBAN

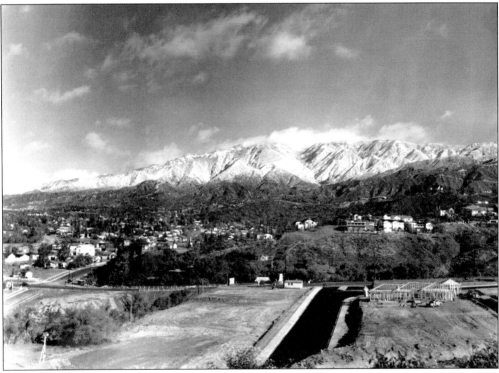

It was a slow shift, but Crescenta Valley was growing out of its rural roots and into a full-fledged suburb. As developers ran out of flat lots to build on, they started to build up. This undated photograph (probably taken in the 1940s) not only shows off the majestic beauty of the snowcapped San Gabriels, but also the beginning of the buildup. The house nearly in the center was the first house on the hills east of Montrose, built in 1928. Today these hills are covered in homes, but the strange politics of the area mean that some of these homes are in Glendale, some in La Cañada, and some in unincorporated La Crescenta. The arch in front of the Indian Springs resort is in the lower center portion of the picture (now occupied by a Vons grocery store). The flat area in the foreground, and indeed that whole neighborhood, is now home to many apartment buildings. (Courtesy Glendale Library.)

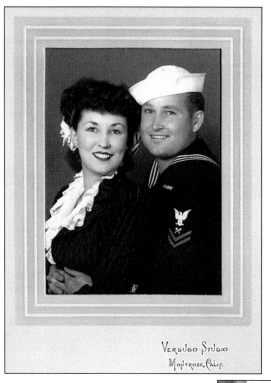

The peaceful life of La Crescenta was interrupted by World War II. A typical Crescent Valley couple, Velma and Tex Farrar pose here for a studio shot at Verdugo Studios mid-war. Tex joined the Navy Sea Bees in the Alutian campaign and the South Pacific. Velma worked at Lockheed in Burbank, building P-38s on swing shift. The family was reunited at war's end and bought a home in Montrose. Their kids grew up in the pleasant small-town atmosphere of the Crescenta Valley, but that house was demolished to make way for the 210 Freeway. (Courtesy Floyd Farrar.)

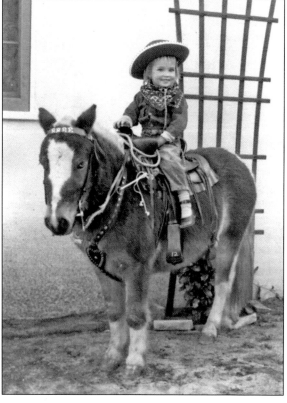

La Crescenta was a great place to be a kid, with plenty of activities at the many parks, Indian Springs swimming pool, Crystal Pool, Montrose Theater, Verdugo Bowl, La Crescenta Bowl, and Onondarka Stables, not to mention the hiking and camping afforded by the mountains. This is three-year-old Carol Farrar playing cowboy in Sparr Heights. (Courtesy Floyd Farrar.)

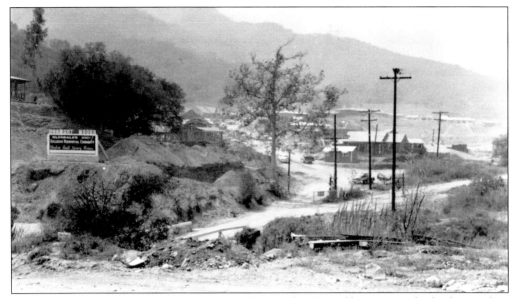

The grounds of the Onondarka ranch were sold around 1950, and houses were built where rodeos were held only a few years earlier. By 1951, many houses had already been completed and more were under construction. The main ranch house was preserved and still stands in the same location today. (Courtesy Glendale Library.)

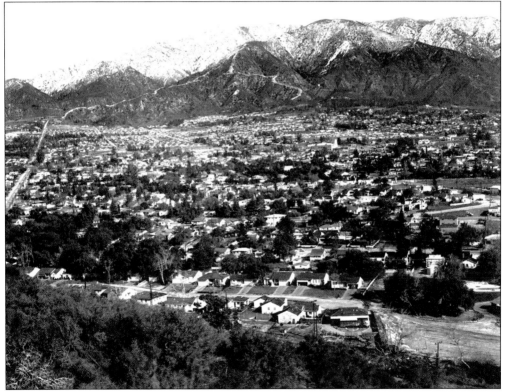

This January 1954 photograph shows how crowded the Crescenta Valley was getting. (Courtesy Glendale Library.)

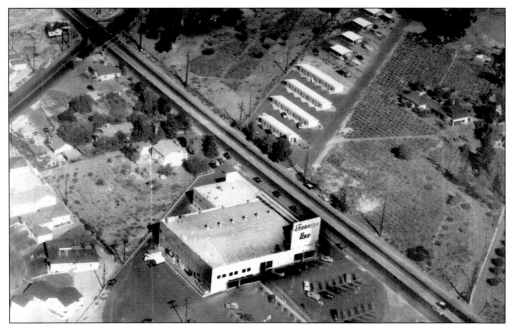

Near the intersection of Foothill Boulevard and Pennsylvania in the late 1940s was the Shopping Bag (now OSH), a deluxe grocery store with a coffee shop and department store on the lower level. Across the street was the Continental Motel, one of several motels along Foothill Boulevard, which was by then Route 118, a main highway that travelers from Route 66 in Pasadena used to get to Oxnard. (Courtesy Glendale Library.)

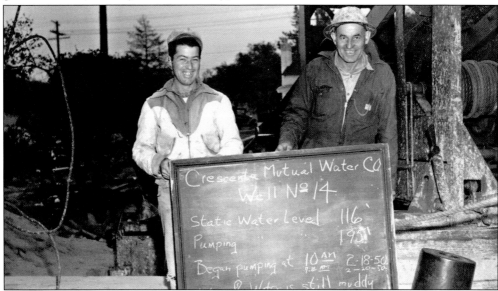

Small water companies came and went in the valley, getting water by tunneling horizontal wells in the mountains. Residents had to buy shares in the local water company that serviced their area. These companies could not supply enough water for the growing population, which lead to the vote that annexed portions of La Crescenta to Glendale. Frank Lanterman solved the water problem with state legislation in 1955, and the Crescenta Valley Water District was formed. (Courtesy Glendale Library.)

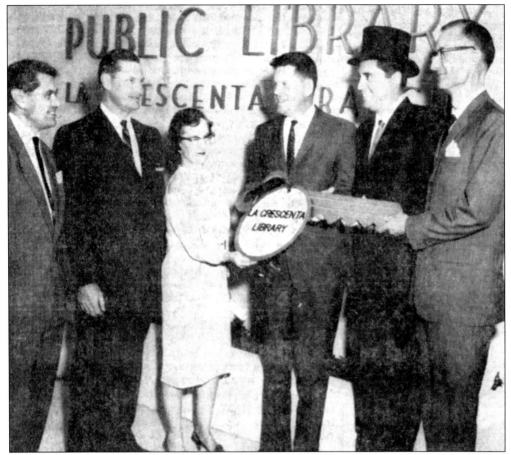

Since 1914, La Crescenta had enjoyed the public library, but was without one after the Glendale annexation in 1951. It took over 10 years and much local activism until local car dealer W. O. Williamson constructed a small building and leased it to the county for use as a library, which is seen here on opening day in 1963.

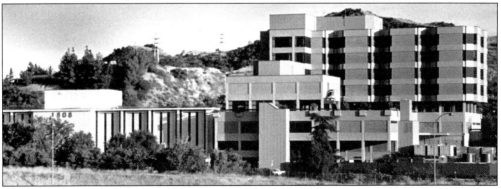

The Verdugo Hills Hospital opened on December 20, 1972, on Verdugo Road, near the Glendale Freeway exit (which wasn't quite finished at the time). The hospital began in 1921 as the Glendale Research Hospital, located on Piedmont Avenue in Glendale. Its services were expanded and, in 1947, the facility was renamed the Behrens Memorial Hospital, after Charles B. Behrens, M.D., who helped plan the health center. (Courtesy Glendale Library.)

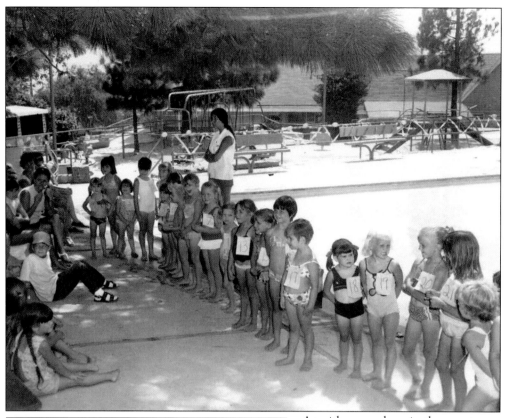

As with everywhere in the country, the baby boom had a huge impact on the Crescenta Valley and prompted the building of more schools and parks. In this 1964 photograph, children are getting ready for swimming class at Dunsmore Park. (Courtesy Glendale Library.)

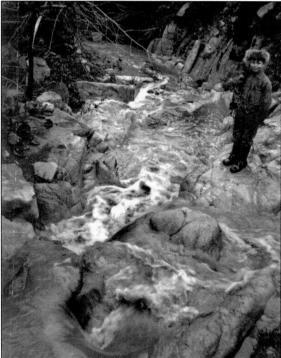

For many decades, children of Crescenta Valley played in the mountains and canyons on their own. Here a boy sporting a Davy Crockett coonskin cap enjoys a raging creek, probably in the late 1950s. Today's parents are reluctant to give their own children the same kind of freedom to explore nature as they had when they were growing up. (Courtesy Glendale Library.)

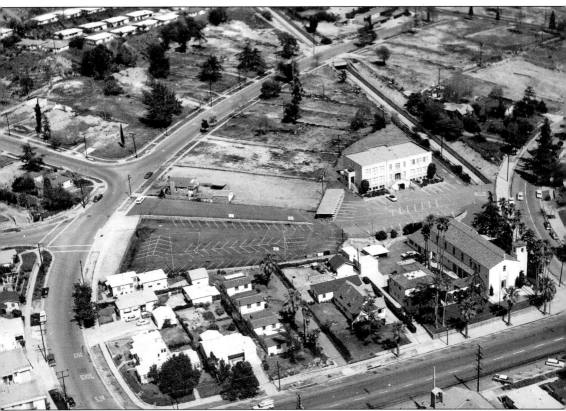

When the state started making plans for building a freeway through the valley, it bought any house that went on the market and left it abandoned, sometimes for years. The designs for the 210 Freeway called for it to cut through the northern most part of Montrose, effectively "pruning" the top portions of the mountain rose street patterns and destroying the original design that the founders had worked so hard to create. This late 1960s photograph shows the swath of empty lots at the northwestern tip of the rose above Florencita and Holy Redeemer Church in the lower right corner. (Courtesy Holy Redeemer.)

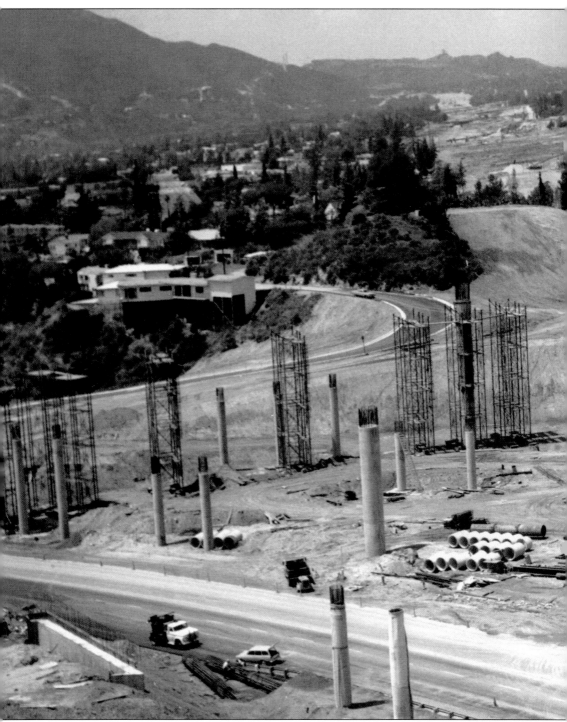

While the freeways are great for getting into and out of the valley, this photograph from around 1972 clearly shows the huge swath of destruction that was necessary to build the 210 Freeway (and ultimately the 2 interchange). The construction was hard on everyone in the area, with constant noise, traffic interruptions, and dirt in the air. Verdugo Road is in the foreground. The

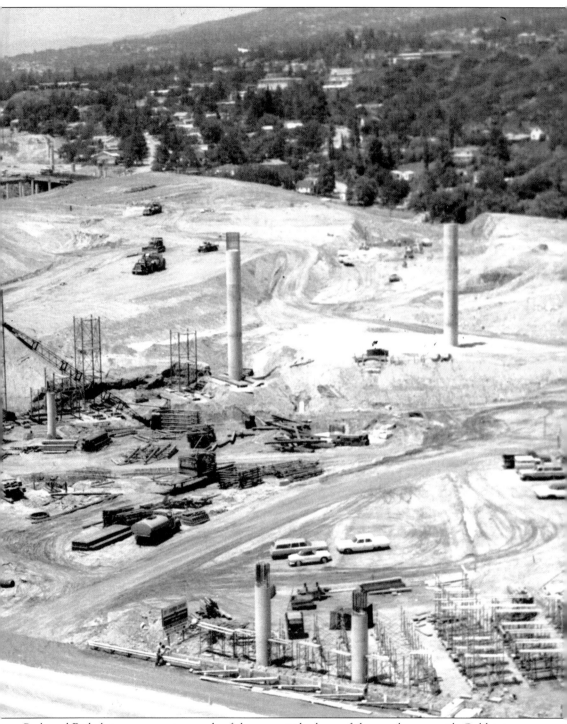
Park-and-Ride lot now occupies much of the area at the base of these columns, with Goldsteins Bagel Factory about where the water truck is and the United Artists movie theatres in La Cañada to the right. (Courtesy Glendale Library.)

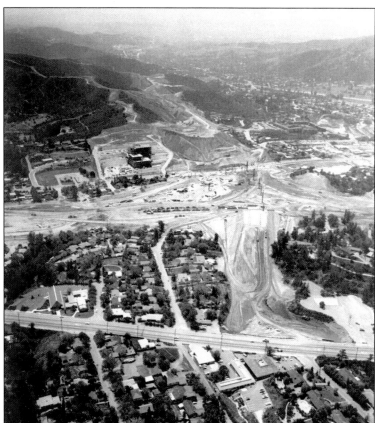

This 1972 photograph shows the early construction of the 2 and 210 Freeways and interchange, including where the 2 ends at Foothill Boulevard. Verdugo Hills Hospital (the large building just off center) is nearly complete and opened later that year. (Courtesy Glendale Library.)

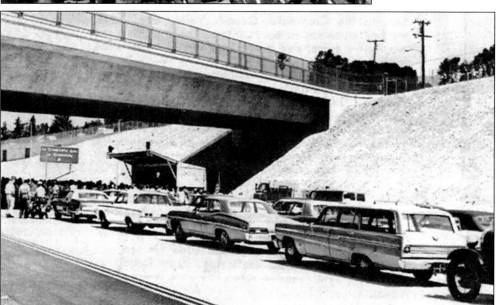

In 1972, an assortment of vintage cars lined the 210 Freeway for its grand opening. Guests gathered under the Ocean View overpass for the festivities. At that time, that stretch of the 210 was only open between Ocean View and Berkshire in La Cañada.

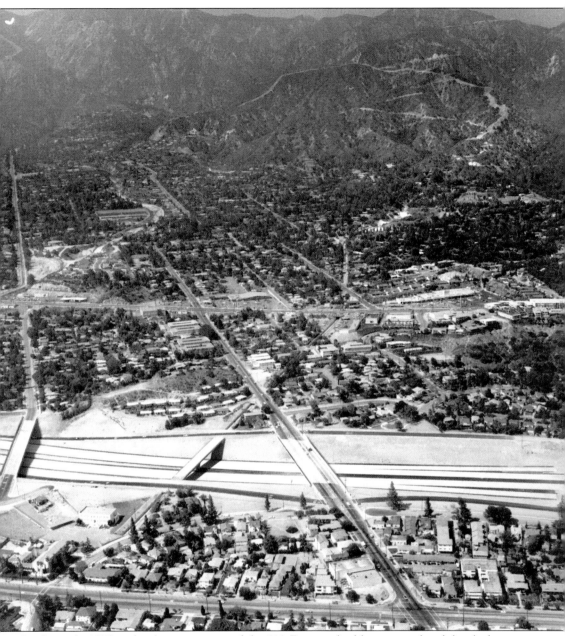

In the early 1970s, after large portions of the 210 Freeway had been completed, but before it opened, the empty freeway was used by movie studios as a location for movies and TV shows like *CHiPs* and *Emergency*. The low-budget, cult classic, Roger Corman film *Death Race 2000* was shot here. Almost every movie or TV show made in the 1970s that had a freeway sequence was shot on this stretch of concrete. Local residents remember constant explosions, fires, and squealing tires during those days. While the 210 was opened between La Cañada and Ocean View in 1972, the 210 did not connect to the I-5 until 1974; the entire stretch from Pasadena to the I-5 was not completed until 1981, giving studios many years of location shooting without having to close working freeways. (Courtesy Glendale Library.)

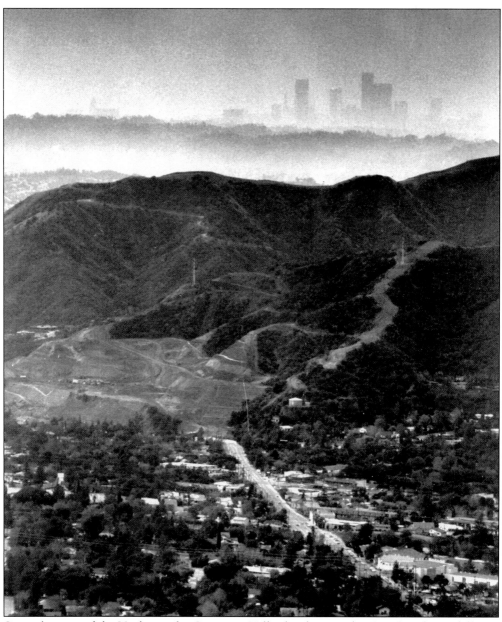

Since the time of the Verdugos, the Crescenta Valley has been tied to Los Angeles in different ways: from the timber being cut from the San Gabriels for L.A., businesses and local grapes being used in L.A. wineries, to other produce being shipped through L.A. to commuters who live in the valley but work in downtown Los Angeles or other parts of the city. This 1979 photograph (taken before the Bunker Hill area in downtown was jammed with skyscrapers) shows just how close the Crescenta Valley is to the central business district of Los Angeles. It also shows the grading for an Oakmont subdivision, as the flatter lands of the valley and relatively flat hilltops have all been built upon, developers have taken to carving into the local mountains to build, destroying the natural beauty of the area. (Locals have stopped more recent subdivisions like this.) With the opening of the 2 Freeway, commuters could make the 14-mile, rush-hour drive to downtown Los Angeles in under 20 minutes. Those days are long gone. (Courtesy Glendale Library.)